Some Excerpts (f

"(2) Your benefit figures shown here are only estimates based on current law, and the laws governing benefit amounts may change because, by 2037, the payroll taxes collected will be enough to pay only about 72 percent of benefits owed." (From "Your Estimated Benefits," issued by the Social Security Administration)

* * * * *

"So the people who are counting on the 'trustees' of the Social Security 'trust' funds are told there is no problem. For example, no problem 'until the year 2037.' The big assumption in those statements is that the trust fund will in fact be paid back."

* * * * *

"There *is* no trust fund. That's because there is no money in it."

* * * * *

"Through 1999, Congress had managed to spend every penny that it could borrow from this Social Security surplus, and had never paid a bit of it back. It enabled them to spend far beyond their own income, to raid the retirement fund, and to keep the public convinced that 'The Budget' was in balance!"

* * * * *

"We have only a limited number of years until the number of retirees surges, by the millions ... But we also need every possible year, between now and when all these people retire, to raise some additional revenue to cover the expected costs of this greatly increased retiree group. There is a one-time window of opportunity right now, but it is closing daily. It is essentially 'now or never.' "

* * * * *

"So get this very clear: the <u>object</u> of getting people to elect privatization is to get people <u>off</u> Social Security <u>so that</u> they are no longer a part of that enormous present impossible future liability ... If the objective is really to eliminate that future liability, plain and simple, *2% isn't going to hack it.*"

BERT H. McLACHLAN is a graduate of Michigan State University and the Harvard Graduate School of Business Administration, and has had a career in corporate controllership and management. He is currently retired from having been the owner of small businesses, and clearly continues to enjoy a fascination with national politics, federal budgeting, Social Security financing and privatization.

SAVING SOCIAL SECURITY
(FROM CONGRESS)

By

BERT H. MCLACHLAN

LEATHERS
PUBLISHING

A division of Squire Publishers, Inc.
4500 College Blvd.
Leawood, KS 66211
1/888/888-7696

Copyright 2001
by Bert McLachlan
All rights reserved

This book, or parts thereof, may not be reproduced in any form without permission.

Printed in the United States

ISBN: 1-58597-082-4

Library of Congress Catalog Card No. 2001 132222

LEATHERS
PUBLISHING

A division of Squire Publishers, Inc.
4500 College Blvd.
Leawood, KS 66211
1/888/888-7696

Introduction

If We Are Wondering about "Saving Social Security," Where Do We Start?

The very words themselves, used for years to con us about Social Security, are all lies: trust fund, trustees, insurance, contributions, earned rights – guaranteed by the law of the land, special bonds, balanced budgets, spending caps, reduced spending, debt reduction, surpluses, even *security*. Every one of them an outright lie! If you believe in the tooth fairy, you'll love the newest bit of (to put it in family-style language) malarkey: "lock boxes." Pure nonsense! The politicians have apparently thought they were safe in assuming that we are all dumb or that we actually like to have the wool pulled over our eyes.

The media chatter these words to us, like parrots or mynah birds, learning to repeat what the Administration tells them, but never knowing what these words mean. Right now, the media chorus (using press release sheet music, and accompanied by the Congressional band) is singing in unison the latest love song about Social Security, "It's all like heaven, 'til 2037." More baloney.

The nation is also still simmering with outrage about Washington, D.C. and what has been going on there. Impeachment, constant "spin," "the politics of personal destruction," and then the recently dragged-out presidential election have lowered politicians even further in the public's

SHOE

Jeff MacNelly/Chicago Tribune Media Services

Social Security is likely to have to start out in a troubled atmosphere.

But even worse than that, our top leaders in Washington can't even seem to agree as to whether there really is a *problem!* The outgoing President has been preaching about "saving" Social Security. But his sidekick assured us, "If it ain't broke, don't fix it!" And the incoming President says it needs to be reformed, presumably meaning that it *can't* be saved. They don't seem to be able to agree on whether there has even been a crime committed in Washington, and the rest of us, out here "beyond the Beltway" are detectives *without a clue* as to what is really going on!

So with dishonest words, a foul political atmosphere, and a clueless public, we are informed that Social Security is going to be put right on the front burner and addressed in the first six months of the new administration. Hold on! Solutions are proposed before anyone even knows the facts, let alone the honest words, and before the nation even understands what the problem is, or whether there is one! We may well be on our way to another Hillary-style decision-making process disaster like the one we went through on health care financing "reform," at the start of the last administration.

Talk about how *not* to handle a problem! Particularly when that problem, Social Security, is the largest financial program in the entire U.S. government. (And it *is* in trouble. Lots of it.) But the way we are going at it is a recipe for outright political disaster.

The main two ingredients for that potential disaster are (1) to repeat, that in large part because of all of the massive lying that has been going on for years about Social Security, *the American public does not have a clue as to what is really going on,* and (2) that the American public can't solve this mystery by picking among suspects before they have even heard the case!

To say it one more way and one more time: On something

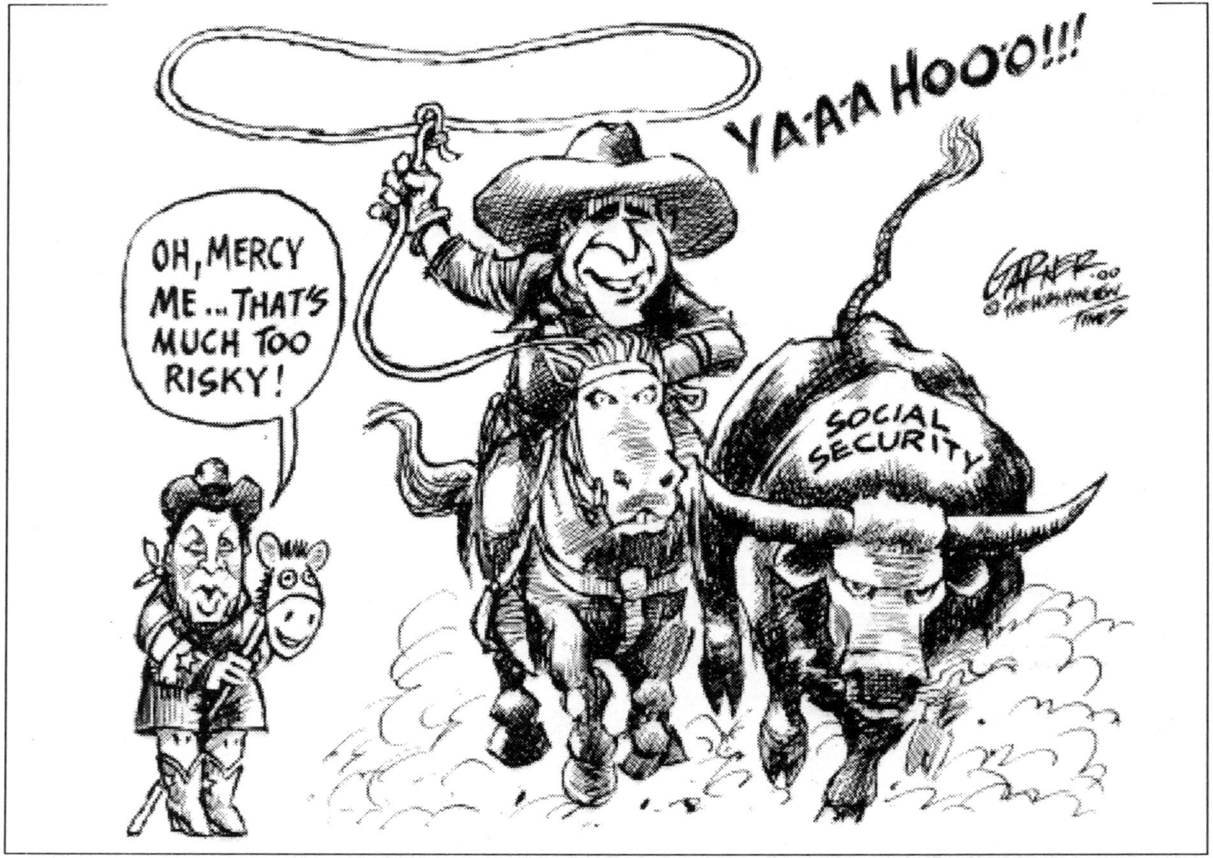
OH, MERCY ME ... THAT'S MUCH TOO RISKY!
YA-A-A HOOO!!!
SOCIAL SECURITY

as enormously important to every one of us as Social Security, we have to use a very careful and thorough decision-making process. That process shouldn't start off by putting the cart in front of the horse: by trying to pick among possible solutions when the process hasn't even dealt with the facts yet. And when it gets to "the facts," we are again back to fact #1: *the American public does not have clue #1 as to what is going on with Social Security!!*

As a presidential candidate, Senator John McCain filled a gargantuan hole of need in our society when he promised us "straight talk." Even if we didn't agree with all his proposed solutions, it was a pure joy to hear a leading politician deal with issues by revealing to us that, in essence, "The Emperor has no clothes!" The nation is sick and tired of both distorted information and the undue influence of a few on our national decision-making.

So, beginning with Social Security, how can we at least start straightening out what is probably our one biggest mess?

It's quite doable. We can do it by simply using a sensible step-by-step decision-making process, by not getting ahead of ourselves in that process, and mainly by educating ourselves as to what the real facts are.

So let's figure out where this decision-making road should begin.

We are not going to start with the history of Social Security. That's water over the dam. And we are not going to review what various benefits are available to you under Social Security. You can call Social Security (at 1-800-772-1213), go to their website (www.ssa.gov), go to their offices, or read their various booklets to get that information. No, we want to start off by looking at Social Security in a broader sense, mainly at its financing and whether it has enough money to pay for what it is promising retirees.

We want to look at where Social Security goes next, and how it is going to get there, because that is going to be up to you.

But first, let's just suppose you are a member of a 10-person group that needs to solve a problem that is important to all of you. The group could be volunteers planning fund raising, or a committee for your union, a community service group, a business advisory board or team, church trustees, an investment club, a political body or the like. In any case, let's also assume that no one of you in the group has any more power than any other, but you need to somehow reach an agreement.

However, the last thing that the group is doing is reaching any agreement. Some members don't really care enough to attend meetings, some deny that any problem even exists, and the others are arguing about what the problem is. One member brought in what she calls "facts," but others don't believe them.

Emotions have run high, and there seem to be all sorts of sub-groups of "us" and "them," based on how differently people see things. At least a couple members are trying to wrap everything up by proposing their own plans, but no one agrees on any of them and one accusation was that, "You're jumping to conclusions!" In fact, there have been some personal attacks.

That's when you stood up, held up your hands, and said, "Wait – a – minute! Hold on! We need to get organized. The only way we are going to solve this is by tackling it <u>step-by-step</u>."

But, to compound the situation, let's assume that, instead of a group of 10, you are dealing with a group of maybe 100 *million*, trying to solve a problem that affects maybe 300 *million* people quite seriously. It has to do with a significant part of their income in that time between when they quit working and when they die. And you thought you had problems with a group of *10*!

But your statement to your group of 10 would also be right for the group of 100 million. The bigger the group, and the more complex the problem, the more it calls for an organized step-by-step process.

We all make decisions every day. What to wear. What to have for breakfast. What to work on today. Which things take priority. How to deal with people. What to watch or not watch on TV. And we make major life decisions, such as about marriage and career, about what to do about Mom and Dad.

Whether we are doing it consciously or unconsciously, we are all using what we can call a "decision-making process," and when more is at stake, we take longer and try to organize the process a little more thoroughly.

By a "decision-making process," we mean that we identify a starting point — where our thinking is now — and then try to figure out those steps that will take us down a road to its end, that end being the decision.

A simplified example of a decision-making process is the selection of a new piece of equipment in a manufacturing company:

1. <u>Recognize a Problem</u> (The present equipment is old and inefficient, with increasing maintenance costs).

2. <u>Gather Facts Bearing on the Problem</u> (Look into what replacement equipment is available, its features, what it costs, how much money each one can save).

3. <u>Discuss and Weigh All These Facts</u> (Compare the various pieces of replacement equipment, and consider the pros and cons of each)

4. <u>Decide on the Criteria, the Rules, the Principles That Will Apply</u> (In this case, the company decides based on whether the equipment will do the needed job and, if so, which equipment pays for itself the soonest by its savings).

5. <u>Reach Conclusions</u> (In this case, narrow it down to those pieces of equipment that will do the job, and pick the one with the best payback).

6. <u>Take Action</u> (Place the order for the equipment, and make plans for removal of the old and installation of the new machinery).

But that oversimplified process, traveling a short and simple road, is totally inadequate for a problem the size of the Social Security system of the United States.

To deal with Social Security, we need to expand that basic 6-step framework above into a series of questions. By then answering those questions, one at a time and in a definite disciplined sequence, we will be taking those steps that get us to the decisions at the end of the much longer Social Security road.

We obviously can't carry out a plan of action until we reach conclusions as to what to do. We also can't be picking among potential conclusions or options until we have absorbed all the facts and weighed them thoroughly. And of course we have to agree on what principles or criteria are most important to use in picking one option versus another.

But, beyond that, we have to go back even further in the process, not only to agree on what the problem is, but also to agree on whether we even *have* a problem.

Then we have to consider who it is that will be responsible for making these decisions about Social Security. The technical answer might be "the President and Congress."

The real answer, though, is that these decisions need to be agreed upon by those who will be affected: the people of the United States themselves. Their senators and representatives are going to vote the way that they know their constituents think and feel, particularly on a subject as sensitive as this.

There will be at least 300 million of us affected by what is decided about Social Security. Some of those 300 million aren't even born yet, but we may be counting on them to grow up, go to work, and pay payroll taxes that enable others of us to retire with our expected benefits. Others are children who are not yet part of the tax-paying workforce. That may leave 200 million of us who could eventually express our choices, but, if presidential elections are any indication, only about half of us will be able to or want to follow this closely enough to express a "vote." So, among the 100 million-or-so of us who might eventually be expressing our opinions on Social Security to our senators and representatives, maybe 60 million or more of us will really be determining the decisions.

That's only 20% of those who will be affected. Only 60 million of the 300 million of us. But the decisions of those 60 million will need to thoughtfully, soberly, even prayerfully address the serious needs of the other 80% or we will have created major, lasting problems, rather than solving them.

So Social Security is an enormous problem, and it is no wonder that politicians have been extremely hesitant to even talk about it.

What we're saying here is that, if we are going to address the subject of Social Security, we will be successful only if millions of us go through a carefully-thought-out decision-making process.

We have to make sure we don't try to "put the cart before the horse." We can't jump to conclusions, or move from X to Y and to Z until we have started with step A and worked our way through each of the steps that is necessary before the next step can be taken.

We will, as a nation, need to move through each single phase in this decision-making process and then stop long enough to make sure we are all still together, before we head on down the road. Some may start "scouting the road ahead" and preparing for the next steps, but the process is not going to work unless we make sure that we are "bringing up the rear" and keeping the group together, on a pace that the whole group can hold, so we all get to the end of the road as one group.

So the first step is to agree on that series of questions which, if answered, will take this nation through the Social Security decision-making process and to answers, whatever they may be.

What follows is both a proposed series of such questions, and also a set of preliminary answers. Hopefully, those initial attempts at answering the questions will be the stimulus for the development of further information, the needed discussion, and eventually enough agreement on the answers that we will be able to keep taking the additional steps that will complete our journey.

The questions are:

1. Are we ready to talk?
2. Where should this fit in the agenda?
3. What exactly *is* the problem?
4. Who should lead this discussion and make the decisions?
5. What should the "code of conduct" for our discussions be?
6. What are the facts about the federal budget?
7. What are the facts about Social Security?
8. What are the facts about investment and "privatization"?
9. What can we learn from other countries?
#10. Should I bail out of Social Security?
#11. But how would we pay for those who stay with Social Security?
#12. So, in summary, what are our options?
#13. What are the principles, the criteria that we will use to decide among these options?
#14. Then what should we do?

Few of us know or care much about accounting and budgets, the difference between "debt" and "deficits," or whatever "compound interest" is. But it is not really all that complicated, if we just go at it slowly and carefully. No one expects you to start out as an expert. But if you will stick with it, you soon *will* be one!

There will be some charts, and there will be some "tables" with lots of numbers in columns. But we will "walk through" those numbers together, so you *do* understand them. Have faith! It's not going to be that hard! Our goal is for all of us to get to the finish line together, with no one left behind.

So let's get at it. Let's start together down that road called "the decision-making process."

CONTENTS

Introduction
    If we are wondering about "Saving Social Security",
    where do we start? i

<u>Questions</u>

\# 1. Are we ready to talk? 1

\# 2. Where should this fit in the agenda? 27

\# 3. What exactly *is* the problem? 31

\# 4. Who should lead this discussion and
     make the decisions? 33

\# 5. What should the "code of conduct" for our discussions be? 37

\# 6. What are the facts about the federal budget? 49

\# 7. What are the facts about Social Security? 89

\# 8. What are the facts about investment and "privatization"? . 127

\# 9. What can we learn from other countries? 155

\#10. Should I bail out of Social Security? 175

\#11. But how would we pay for those who stay with
     Social Security? 195

\#12. So, in summary, what are our options? 211

\#13. What are the principles, the criteria that we will use
     to decide among these options? 235

\#14. Then what should we do? 241

Question #1

Are We Ready to Talk?

Is there really a problem? Is Social Security enough of a problem that we should focus our attention on it now? Those are not really simple questions with a simple answer.

There are certainly those who have been saying that the time has come to talk about Social Security:

> "Social Security...is not actuarially sound; it promises more benefits to more people than the income or premiums collected will provide. By no stretch of the imagination can it be called an insurance program.
>
> "Supporters of Social Security speak of the trust fund when, in fact, there is no trust fund. It is a bookkeeping deception. The actual monies collected under the Social Security tax law go into the general Treasury of the United States. This has been true since the inception of the program, and the monies have been spent each year. The so-called trust fund is no more than a promissory note from the government of the United States to the bookkeepers of the Social Security system to honor their demand on the Treasury of the United States."

That was said in 1964. Thirty-seven years ago. By Barry

Goldwater, speaking out on Social Security while campaigning unsuccessfully against Lyndon Johnson for the presidency.

It isn't as if this is a new subject, or that no one has been trying to focus our attention on it.

"It is time for social security to be reevaluated and fundamentally reformed.

"In addition, the social security program has long been misrepresented and deceptively described by politicians and government officials in order to create a false impression among voters about the true nature and operation of the program. This false impression has been used to cover up many of the program's major shortcomings and to sell it to a public that would probably not buy it if it understood how it really worked.

"Economist Arthur Laffer has compared social security to a red Maserati racing toward a brick wall at 100 miles an hour. It will be stopped; the only question is in what shape. We will either reform social security now, or we will restructure the program out of the salvaged wreckage.

"Basic and fundamental reform of social security is inevitable because the program cannot continue as it is.

"To pay the benefits currently being promised to young workers entering the work force today, tax rates will have to be raised to between 25% to 33% of the taxable payroll, as compared with 12% today.

"...given the current climate of public opinion taxpayers will probably not be willing to pay the enormous tax increases necessary to bail out the program.

"When taxpayers finally will tolerate no more, when the program threatens to collapse into bankruptcy, when voters finally learn the truth, basic and fundamental changes in the program will have to be made. It seems that sooner or later one or more of these events will occur, and when they do social security will fall."

Those excerpts come from a book written 21 years ago, in 1980, by Peter J. Ferrara: "Social Security, The Inherent Contradiction." He saw it clearly, even back then, and spelled it out in far more detail than even those excerpts indicate. And he has kept trying to spread that message ever since.

"The most serious threat to Social Security in the immediate future is the widespread misunderstanding of the program...... *The Social Security program is not what most people think it is.*"

"The only reverence we owe these past decisions is to fulfill the promises made to date to our older population. It is entirely reasonable, therefore, that we give serious consideration to a completely new type of social insurance system for the relatively young segment of our population, even if we continue the present system for the older segment of the population.

"The (U.S. Social Security) system is in place, and if it is not changed, it will almost certainly require payroll tax rates of two to three times today's levels.

"Not only are Social Security benefits not *paid for* by the government, they are not *guaranteed* by the government.

"The public can no longer be tranquilized by public relations campaigns about how good Social Security is; it is time to develop solutions to the problems."

Those excerpts came from a book written in 1981, with the title, "The Coming Revolution in Social Security." Did the author know what he was talking about? He certainly should have, because he was A. Haeworth Robertson, and he had been the Chief Actuary of the United States Social Security Administration from 1975 to 1978, after which his continuing concern about these problems led him to form and lead the Retirement Policy Institute.

In 1986, Michael Boskin, in his "Too Many Promises: The Uncertain Future of Social Security" told us,

"The best time to deal with the crisis looming in the future is now — before we reach the precipice. If we do not make structural changes in Social Security soon, our options will be sharply limited, our ability to respond to crises without major disruption will decrease, and the opportunity to set a sound future course for our most significant social program will rapidly slip away as the baby boom generation approaches retirement."

He was telling us that 15 years ago.

"Imagine walking into your congressman's office with irrefutable evidence that the United States in the next century will face a possibly ruinous economic and social crisis. You assure your representative, however, that opportunities exist to take early corrective action to head off this impending disaster. Your optimism that such action will occur is dampened when you tell your congressman what issues are involved. Social Security? Forget it. The senior citizen organizations won't allow Congress even to discuss the issue. The federal deficit? It's a no-win topic. Private pension policy? It's boring, a non-vote getter. Because of its politically unappealing nature, the most critical economic issue America will face in the twenty-first century continues to simmer unabated.

"The pending crisis....."

"Sooner or later, though, we're going to have to face facts. Sooner would be better.

"Changes in the financing of retirement are inevitable with Social Security, because there will not be enough money to pay the promised benefits..."

The earlier of the excerpts above came from a chapter titled, "The Mess We Are In." Some other headings in the book were "Enduring Myths," "A War Between the Generations?" and "How Privatization Might Work." The book was written ten years ago, in 1991, and is called "Social Insecurity, The Crisis in America's Social Security System and How to Plan Now for Your Own Financial Survival." The author? Dorcas R. Hardy, who was U.S. Commissioner of Social Security under presidents Reagan and Bush after serving as assistant secretary of Health and Human Services, where she supervised programs for the elderly.

It was back in 1994 that the now-famous Third Millennium survey found that 46% of 18 to 34-year-olds seriously thought UFOs exist, but only 28% of them thought Social Security would exist by the time they retired.

In January 1995, Senators Robert Kerrey and John Danforth submitted the Final Report of the Bipartisan Commission on Entitlement and Tax Reform to President Clinton. That Final Report cited the commission's earlier 1994 Interim Report, saying that it was:

> "...a stark call to action, alerting Americans about the burden that is being shifted to future generations, about the deteriorating national savings rate, the squeezing out of public funds for essential and appropriate government investment, and the impending insolvency of both the Social Security and Medicare Trust Funds."

The final four recommendations of the commission in early 1995 were:

> "Second, current laws must be changed to create a future in which we balance our entitlement commitments and the funds available to honor those promises. This is important for generational equity.

> "Third, we must empower the American people to participate in developing satisfactory solutions. Washington does not have all of the answers and unless the public participates, reform will not take place until more dramatic solutions are required.

> "Fourth, the Administration and Congress should consider reform of the tax system.

> "Fifth, the Commission, in this Final Report, restates its plea for *immediate* action on reform."

But they didn't get it. For one thing, the 30 members of the Commission couldn't agree at all on how to carry out those general objectives.

A cover article in TIME magazine, March 20, 1995, was "The Case for Killing Social Security." The article concluded perceptively, "The problem is the sort that representative governments are not good at solving: a potential disaster that can be clearly foreseen but is not imminent, and that can be escaped only by accepting some present pain as the price of avoiding much worse future pain..... Whether both parties can overcome the impulse to demagoguery and agree on some reasonable reforms poses nothing less than a severe test of democratic government."

By 1996, Marshall Carter and Bill Shipman wrote probably the clearest explanation yet of the problems and potential solutions for Social Security. Bill Shipman was and is still one of the two co-chairmen of the Cato Institute's Project on Social Security Privatization. The 1996 book was, "Promises to Keep: Saving Social Security's Dream." Among other things, the book noted:

"America's Social Security system and similar programs in other countries are in serious trouble. These systems, while originally well intentioned, are irredeemably flawed in design. They are underfunded, face increasing demands from aging populations, and are headed for insolvency in the first quarter of the twenty-first century."

But they also introduced a note of new optimism:

"Throughout the country there is a growing consensus among Americans of varying ages, economic classes, and political parties that we can no longer rely upon Social Security to provide a secure retirement for the elderly."

And they may have signaled an evolution on the subject:

> "So we must have the courage to change. The question is what sort of change is most appropriate."

Also in 1996, Sam Beard, in his "Restoring Hope in America: the Social Security Solution," concluded, "The need to get reforms underway is urgent. There is only a five-to-eight-year window within which we can afford to change the Social Security system and create the personal investment and retirement accounts I describe.....Together, we can become a mighty force for change. But we need to act now."

By 1998, Edward Gramlich, who had chaired the Social Security Advisory Council from 1994 to 1997, wrote "Is It Time to Reform Social Security?," and his answer was, "Yes."

Also in 1998, Martin Feldstein, a Harvard economics professor and president of the National Bureau of Economic Research, edited "Privatizing Social Security," a collection of ten papers on the subject. In his preface he noted:

> "This volume focuses on the possible methods and problems involved in shifting from an unfunded system of social security retirement benefits to a system based on mandatory saving in individual accounts. The research project that led to the current volume began several years ago. It is interesting to note that, when the project began, there were many who were quite skeptical about whether this was even a subject worth studying since the idea of such a radical change in the form of social security financing seemed so politically implausible. Much has changed since then."

And in 1999, in the midst of ever-escalating discussion of reform of Social Security, Steve Forbes began his second campaign for President and summarized his policies in "A New Birth of Freedom." He pointed out that as far back as 1984, in Forbes magazine, he had written, "Social Security's long-term finances are...a disaster." In addition to favoring personal retirement accounts for younger workers, he concluded, "*Fifth, we must start right away, while we still have time.*"

You might think of all of these above-mentioned writers as being like a group of canoeists floating along on a quiet river in their canoes. But they are experienced at what they are doing, they listen better than the rest of us, and they hear a big waterfall coming up ahead.

We certainly can't say we haven't been told, or that we haven't been warned for a long time. But are enough of us listening or believing what we are hearing? The people quoted above would certainly have their doubts.

But they should have continuing faith, because the subject of Social Security is in fact "coming to a head."

By July 1999, when a Wall Street Journal/NBC News Poll asked Americans whether they were dissatisfied or satisfied with how Congress was handling certain legislative priorities, the major dissatisfaction was expressed on "Reforming Social Security": 69% of Americans said they were dissatisfied, and only 19% said they were satisfied. (The next highest level of dissatisfaction was on "Reforming Medicare," where the respective percentages were 64% and 19%.)

The American public is, in fact, quite awake to this subject, and strongly (7 out of 10 of us) dissatisfied with the way Congress is handling it (or *failing* to handle it).

Also, as quoted in TIME magazine, February 28, 2000, a poll taken by Opinion Research Corp. International for Nationwide Insurance concluded that most Americans are optimistic that the economy will keep growing but have plenty of anxiety about their financial situation. The #1 item on the list of things that people said they fear was, "The Social Security system will falter or fail before their retirement." 56% indicated that fear. The public is clearly waking up to the seriousness of this issue.

Bill Clinton has, as President, certainly shown himself to be sensitive to which way the winds are blowing politically in the U.S. So when he submitted his budget for fiscal 2001 to Congress in February, 2000, he was acknowledging the evolution in our readiness to deal with Social Security when the budget message devoted two entire pages to "Saving Social Security," saying in part:

> "Restoring the Social Security trust funds to long-range solvency is one of the President's top priorities. He led the way in 1998 with a series of regional bipartisan forums to build public awareness of the problem, and to build public consensus for solutions. In 1999, the President proposed a framework built on the principle of maintaining long-term fiscal responsibility – ensuring that the benefits of fiscal discipline be used to extend the life of Social Security while also making prudent investments in activities that enhance the Nation's economic performance. Such a framework is crucial, because the Government's ability to pay future Social Security benefits is tightly linked to the long-term economic and budgetary outlook.
>
> "This year, the President urges the Congress to adopt his program to save Social Security through a commitment to sustained fiscal responsibility."

President Clinton also popularized the slogan, "Saving Social Security," although when it got right down to specific proposals to do the "saving," he apparently felt safe only in ad-

Steve Kelley, San Diego Union-Tribune, Copley News Service

vancing the general proposition of fiscal responsibility.

He did float a trial balloon about having the government invest in corporate bonds and stocks, but that one was quickly (and appropriately) shot down. The dangers of having the government owning large parts of U.S. business were clear, and that proposal can happily be considered as now eliminated from the agenda. But his proposal was at least an acknowledgment of the truth that better returns can be realized from actual investment in profit-making businesses.

He deserves credit for reading the times correctly, advancing awareness of the problem, and getting us ready to finally deal with it.

And President George W. Bush also sensed the mood of the nation by having made it a central part of his presidential campaign to promise to reform Social Security. When he grabbed "the 3rd rail of politics," he wasn't electrocuted (as everyone predicted for any politician who actually touched the Social Security reform issue), but elected.

He promised, "Returning Social Security to sound financial

footing will be one of my highest priorities. I'll strengthen Social Security so government keeps its promises to America's seniors, while at the same time allowing younger Americans the choice to voluntarily invest some of their Social Security taxes in personal accounts." He then went on to spell out a specific program to build bipartisan consensus based on six principles.

Unfortunately, though, that still doesn't mean that the nation is ready yet to really talk about Social Security.

Bush was hardly elected before Business Week magazine was saying, "And Social Security reform? Don't expect it any time soon." The article went on to say, "Many moderate Democrats back private accounts, but the idea will generate a firestorm of opposition from labor and party liberals," and to quote former Congressional Budget Office Director Robert D. Reischauer as saying, "When the details come out, it's going to be very controversial."

The Christian Science Monitor weighed in with a front-page article on the Bush agenda, noting that "Social Security reform could be a tough sell for the Bush team.....Attempts to reform Social Security have traditionally met resistance in Congress."

And even the Wall Street Journal, within weeks of Bush's election, was headlining an article, "Bush Plan to Privatize Social Security Will Face Host of Hurdles," and contending, "Mr. Bush may well find that the election was the easy part. Turning his Social Security campaign pledge into government policy promises to be a long and difficult challenge."

So are we ready to talk about Social Security or not?

One advantage of our form of government is that it can keep inappropriate change from happening too fast or without adequate support. The other side of the coin is of course that the system can fail to move fast enough when there is a real problem that the public doesn't yet understand or accept.

In the late 1930s, the Nazi military forces were overrunning

Europe and the Japanese were ravaging China and Southeast Asia. But it took the December 7, 1941 bombing of Pearl Harbor in Hawaii to finally get the attention of the American public and to wake us up to the fact that we had to act.

It took at least thirty years of having the welfare policies of the "Great Society" devastate urban families, and a change in control of Congress before we faced the fact that welfare really *did* need to be reformed. We were getting what we paid for, and it wasn't what we had expected. But it took us a *long* time to realize that, and so it will be a *long* time before we recover from what we had done.

The very positive oddity about the present perception of the Social Security problems is that the nation appears to be far less afraid of the subject than the politicians are.

There are many examples of our readiness to deal with Social Security in a poll conducted by Zogby International in July, 1999. Some of those examples are:

"For instance, 44.7% of union members and 42.3% of non-union members agree that the current social security system is more risky than privatization because the government cannot pay all of the benefits.

"Presidential and Congressional candidates who support privatization are more likely to attract voters than those who do not support it.

"Union members, Hispanics and African-Americans (all Democrats traditionally), are entertaining the concept of private investment of at least some of their taxes.

"Interestingly, awareness of the debate declines with age....

"When asked, 'Would you prefer or not prefer that the Social Security system be changed to give those who want the choice of investing their Social Security taxes through individual accounts similar to IRAs or 401(k) programs?', these were the answers by age group:

	18-29	30-49	50-64	65+	Overall
Prefer	78.3%	71.0%	51.4%	26.5%	54.9%
Not prefer	12.6%	17.7%	35.3%	53.8%	31.4%
Not sure	9.1%	11.3%	13.4%	19.7%	13.8%

One venture at interpreting those results would be that (1) those 65 and over might well not prefer such a change because of uncertainty as to how it might affect *their* retirement income to have some people no longer providing payroll tax income for Social Security, and that (2) having about one out of seven (13.8%) of those who answered be "not sure" is a very sensible response at this point.

But there is clearly a preference for some "privatization" option by more than half of those 64 and younger, and a very strong preference for that option by those 49 and younger.

It actually looks as if it might be a "no brainer" for politicians to at least now be ready to *talk* about Social Security. It appears that the rest of us *already* are.

Another little checkpoint is that apparently 57% of those who were asked in exit polls during the last presidential election said they favored private accounts.

Another checkpoint might be to see what the trustees of the Social Security trust funds concluded in their most recent annual report. After noting that there had been better economic performance in recent years, they then said:

"But as we noted earlier, a few good years do not reduce the inherent uncertainty about the future. We sincerely hope that the debate about the future of Social Security continues and provides the information base for the public to decide soon what kind of changes they believe will serve them best."

The trustees are saying that they do want us to discuss this. In fact, if their report were less formal, they might well have said, "If you have understood what you have just read, you know you'd darn well *better* discuss it!"

All of that tells you what "the experts" think about this. But you yourself should probably look at at least three basic pieces of information about Social Security. Those are (1) what the trustees of Social Security and Medicare think our payroll taxes will be if we stay on the course we're on, (2) the "demographic" shifts (changes in our population, by age groups) that are the basic inescapable major cause of these problems, and therefore (3) the predictable changes in the ratio of workers to retirees.

When you have reviewed those three pieces of information, you will have to come up with your *own* answer to the question, "Are we ready to talk?"

First, what the trustees tell us about expected payroll taxes.

Projected Payroll Tax Rates

For openers, we need to clarify what we are talking about when we say "Social Security" or "Medicare."

These two general programs get their income mainly from what we call the "FICA tax," or payroll tax. Actually, half of it is paid by the employee out of his or her salary or wages, and the other half is paid by the employer. In truth, the employer pays these taxes only when it is necessary to pay an employee (and deducts equal amounts from the employee's pay).

But the government taxes half of this money one way and

Saving Social Security (from Congress)

"I have before me, gentlemen, some figures that may shock you, as they did me."

half of it another way. For the *employer*, anything that the company pays as a direct tax (such as the company's half of the FICA tax) is treated the same way on the company's tax return as any salary or wages paid to an employee: it is all deductible expense for the employer, when the income tax is figured. But for the *employee*, the FICA tax is (1) taken out of his or her pay as a tax, but is (2) then also counted as "income" when the employee calculates taxable income for the year. So employers, economists and realists all consider the FICA tax as one total which would be considered as all coming out of the employee's pay, if it weren't for the way the IRS figures income tax.

In any case, "FICA" (in some clever wording, as we'll cover later) stands for "Federal Insurance Contributions Act." This FICA, or payroll tax, totals to 15.30% of taxable payroll, comes out of both the employee and employer, goes to the IRS, and then gets distributed this way:

	From the Employee	From the Employer	Total Tax
1. Goes to the "OASI" fund in Social Security, for retirement benefits, including survivors benefits:	5.30%	5.30%	10.60%
2. Goes to the "DI" fund in Social Security, for disability insurance:	0.90%	0.90%	1.80%
3. Goes to Medicare, Part A, the hospital fund, or the "HI" fund:	1.45%	1.45%	2.90%
TOTAL	7.65%	7.65%	15.30%

So the money collected as "payroll tax" goes in three different directions, to three different funds.

Just to get a general overall picture of how these three programs are doing in total, or expected to do in the future, let's look at one small part of the year 2000 annual report of the trustees of these funds, to see how Social Security and Medicare are expected to do in total.

The same six people are trustees for all the funds. In their annual report, the trustees of the Social Security retirement and survivors insurance fund (OASI), disability insurance fund (DI) and hospital insurance fund (HI) total up the three of these (then called OASDI + HI) funds and show their expectations in total for the three through the year 2075, in three categories: (1) optimistic estimates, (2) intermediate estimates, and (3) pessimistic estimates. As we'll cover in more detail as we go along, an unbelievable amount of analysis and calculation goes into producing this information, which is the best that anyone can come up with.

To try to simplify the presentation of the projections that the trustees have made, through the year 2075, as to how these three funds will do in total, Chart #1-1, on page 19 leaves off the "optimistic" projections and concentrates on (1) what the trustees expect, as an average or "intermediate" forecast of the future, and (2) what they think might be the "pessimistic" forecast. We are concentrating on the middle-of-the-road or down side of the expectations, to be sure we can handle those.

So on Chart #1-1 there are four lines. The two _solid_ lines show the "intermediate" forecast, the lower line being the forecasted cash _income_ of these funds and the upper line of the two being the forecasted cash _outgo_ (or expenses) of these funds, in total. Likewise, the two _dash_ lines are the "pessimistic" forecast, with the lower line again being the income and the upper line being the outgo.

Are We Ready to Talk?

CHART 1-1: OASDI + HI (Old-Age, Survivors, Disability and Medicare) Funds, Total. Forecasts by the Fund Trustees in the Year 2000 to the Year 2075. Calendar Years, with income excluding interest income.

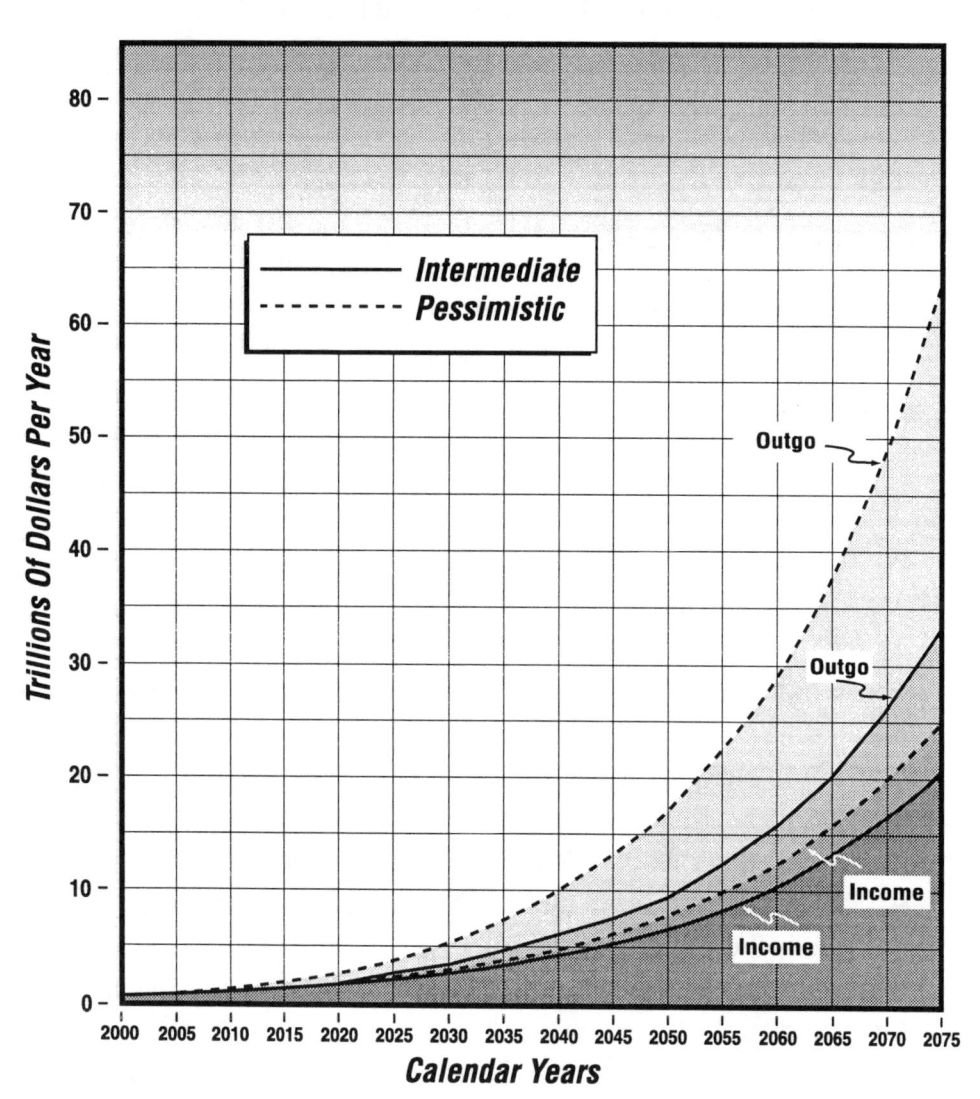

——— Intermediate Forecast   ------------ Pessimistic Forecast

Source: Pages 183-4, The 2000 Annual Report of the Board of Trustees of the Federal Old-Age and Survivors Insurance and Disability Insurance Trust Funds, U.S. Government Printing Office

On the left side of the chart, you can see that we are talking about <u>trillions</u> of dollars per year, and on the bottom scale of the chart, from left to right, we are looking at the years from 2000 through 2075. (A trillion is one thousand billions).

Let's review, first, what the two solid lines say about the "intermediate" forecast.

The difference between those two solid lines is the amount by which the outgo will exceed the income. By the year 2035, that amount is $1 trillion 416 billion per year. By the year 2075, it is $12 trillion 223 billion per year. Well, yes, those are in future dollars, which will be inflated from the value of present dollars, so let's translate that into percent of taxable income.

In 2075, the income (per the solid "intermediate" line) would be 16.74% of taxable payroll, and the outgo, the "cost rate" would be <u>26.21% of payroll!</u> The income would fall short of the outgo by 9.47% of payroll.

So if that isn't bad enough to get our attention, let's look at the "pessimistic" forecast, as shown by the two dash lines (top line, outgo, and lower dash line, income). In this case, the outgo by the year 2035 would exceed the income by some $3 trillion 633 billion per year. By the year 2075, the outgo would exceed the income by <u>$37 trillion 391 billion</u> per year. In payroll tax terms, that would be income of 17.41% of taxable payroll, and outgo of <u>42.16% of payroll!</u> The income would fall short of the outgo by 24.74% of payroll. Or to say it another way, for every dollar of expected outgo, there would be only 40 cents of income.

This is the best available information from our best experts, and the prediction — whether "intermediate" or "pessimistic" is for total disaster.

Maybe we *do* need to talk about Social Security and Medicare. And later, we need to talk about whether we can handle all of this subject area at once, or whether we need to take one thing at a time.

Changes in our population, by age groups

Secondly, (after looking at the expected impossible payroll taxes), you need to look at the demographic shifts (the changes in our population, by age groups).

These changes can be predicted with a tremendous degree of accuracy. We know how many of us are alive and of what ages. We know how many are being born and how long we are living. We know how many will be of working age and how many of us will be in the retirement years.

Let's analyze the specific estimates of the number of people who will be working (and therefore paying payroll taxes into Social Security) and the number of people who will be retired (and therefore drawing their retirement income from Social Security). This is called "the dependency ratio."

(There are, incidentally, those who say we should be looking at a "total" dependency ratio, that being the ratio of the number of people working to a total of [1] the youngsters, not yet working, *plus* [2] the number of people retired. They say *that* ratio hasn't changed so much. But government reports show that the cost of maintaining a retiree is many, many times that of a child. The generally-accepted measure is the dependency ratio: workers to retirees.)

So let's look at a 35-year span from 1995 to the year 2030:

These numbers come out of the last annual report of the Social Security trustees. This is their "intermediate" estimate, or middle-of-the-road expectation (in thousands of people):

Year	Workers	Beneficiaries
1995	141,087	37,376
	+12,473	+ 817
2000	153,560	38,193
	+ 5,714	+ 1,957
2005	159,274	40,150
	+ 5,626	+ 3,776
2010	164,900	43,926
	+ 4,223	+ 6,131
2015	169,123	50,057
	+ 2,812	+ 7,509
2020	171,935	57,566
	+ 2,013	+ 7,194
2025	173,948	64,760
	+ 2,178	+ 5,797
2030	176,126	70,557

Let's be sure we understand what those numbers can tell us. To begin with, in 1995 we had 141 million workers supporting 37 million retirees (or "beneficiaries"). Then in the next 5 years (between 1995 and the year 2000), we added more than 12 million workers but less than 1 million retirees. Fine. We are adding a lot of people to the group that pays the bill (the workers), while adding very few to the group that gets the benefits (the retirees).

In the 5 years from 2000 to 2005, and again in the 5 years from 2005 to 2010, we keep on adding more workers than we do retirees. (So we are, as a matter of fact, collecting *far* more than we are spending in those years).

But notice how it changes in the 5 years from 2010 to 2015. Now it is going the other way. In those 5 years, we expect to add more than 6 million retirees but only about 4 million more workers.

In the 5 years from 2015 to 2020, though, and again in the 5 years after that (from 2020 to 2025), the shift is even greater. From 2015 to 2020, we expect to add only 2 million 800 thousand workers but 7 million 500 thousand retirees. And from 2020 to 2025, we expect to add only 2 million workers and 7 million 194 thousand retirees.

In the years from 2025 to 2030, you can see that this addition of more retirees than workers goes on "big time," and although you don't see the further numbers, the projections through the year 2075 continue to show that we will keep adding more retirees than workers. For every beneficiary that we add, starting somewhere around the year 2010, we will be adding less than one worker.

In those same numbers, we can summarize that in the 20 years from 2010 to 2030 we will add only 11 million 226 thousand workers, but 26 million 631 retirees. There are obviously going to be less and less workers supporting more and more retirees.

The ratio of workers to retirees

If you don't grasp the enormous significance of that second piece of information (the "demographic" shifts), it may help to then look at the third piece of information, which is, in fact, from that same demographic information, but now showing it as the number of workers paying payroll taxes, as a ratio, compared to the number of beneficiaries.

That ratio shows on Chart 1-2, page 24, and is very important for all of us to understand.

The year 1945 (very soon after Social Security started paying retirement benefits) is way off the chart. Back then, there were 42 workers for every one retired. On average, few people lived beyond 65 in those days. No problem paying their retirement benefits.

24 SAVING SOCIAL SECURITY (FROM CONGRESS)

CHART 1-2: Pertaining to OASI (Retirement and Survivors Insurance, but not Disability Insurance): Number of Workers Paying Payroll Taxes for Every Beneficiary (Retiree Drawing Benefits). Intermediate Estimate

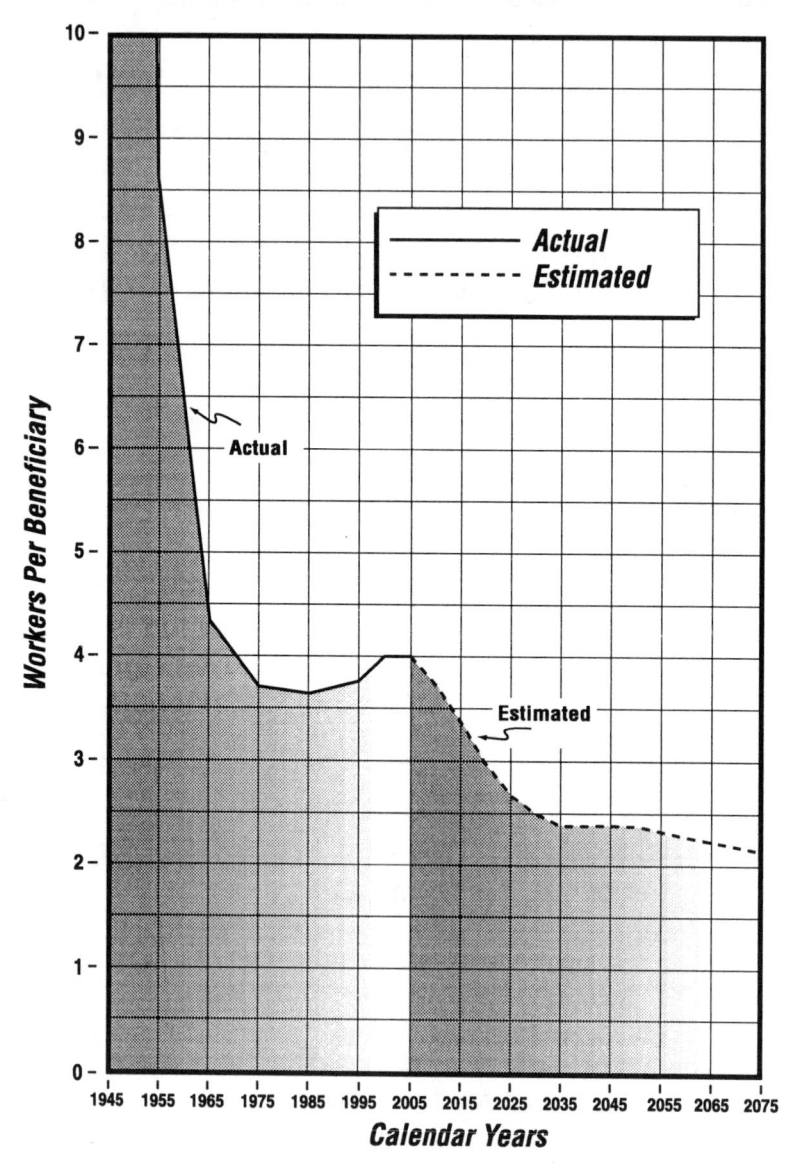

Source: Page 122, The 2000 Annual Report of the Board of Trustees of the Federal Old-Age and Survivors Insurance and Disability Insurance Trust Funds, U.S. Government Printing Office.

By 1950, the number was down from 42 to 16.5, and by 1955 the line comes onto the chart, showing us that by then we were down to having only 8.6 workers supporting each retiree. Still not a big problem.

But by 1970, we were now down to only 4.1 workers per retiree, and the ratio got down to 3.7 in 1985, before it came back up to a present level of around 4 workers per retiree drawing retirement benefits.

But from here, it's all downhill.

This "intermediate" estimate shows the expected number of workers per retiree to be headed down toward 2.16 in the year 2075. And the "pessimistic" estimate, which isn't included on this chart, would be a line that keeps getting a little further below the "intermediate" line until it gets down to *1.59* in the year 2075. Beyond that, both the intermediate and pessimistic estimates keep getting *worse.*

Stop and think about that. Really think about it, because you have arrived at the heart of the problem and it is inescapable.

We are headed toward a time when about 2 or less of us support each retiree.

You may think of it as a husband and wife supporting a retiree. Here, we are looking at only the retirement income, but the additional aspect of it is that (as we looked at earlier) these same 2 (or less) people will have to be paying all of those medical bills, too. Two people (or less) paying for themselves and their children *and* all of the retirement income *and* medical bills for one retiree. Themselves, without help.

You now can understand that, by the intermediate forecast, a ratio of 2 workers per retiree is absolutely impossible, and that, by the pessimistic forecast, a ratio of about 1.6 workers per retiree is even *more* absolutely impossible.

If your reaction is "oh, my god," then you've got it. You have joined the ranks of those who understand the problem. There may be other details, but you've got the picture. You, too, can hear the waterfall.

Maybe when enough of us have this understanding, we will reach a consensus that it is at least time to *talk* about Social Security reform.

But if *do* reach that consensus, we then come to the question of how much we can handle at once.

Question #2

Where Should This Fit in the Agenda?

We may be ready to talk about "Social Security," but first we need to be sure of what we are talking about. Then we have to decide what priority to give it, in that there are lots of other things also on the agenda in Washington.

When that "FICA" or payroll tax is taken out of your pay, it goes in those three directions: (1) the retirement plan, (2) disability insurance, and (3) Medicare. As you will recall, those are called OASI, DI, and HI in government lingo.

To begin with, all of that, as one big topic, is impossible to tackle at once. The three programs have entirely separate problems. If you think there have been problems in facing up to even the crisis in the retirement plan, you have to realize that there are even bigger problems in facing up to the costs of the financing of medical care for seniors (both through Medicare and Medicaid).

The topics certainly have to be taken one at a time, and so the proposal here is that we deal with only the retirement income plan (OASI) and, for now, leave the problems of disability insurance and Medicare for another day. Optimistically, if we show that we as a nation can deal with the problems of the retirement income plan, then maybe we will have established a format that we can use to tackle the problems of disability insurance and medical care financing for seniors.

So from here on out, we are talking about working on the problems of only OASI, the retirement income plan.

Others may well disagree, and that is why this is a question that must be addressed.

The politicians already have full plates. The last presidential campaign focused on education. Campaign finance reform got a lot of mention. Prescription drugs were an issue. Tax cuts were a major item, and national security and defense didn't seem to be of much interest. There are campaign promises to be kept.

With 100 senators and 435 representatives, there are bound to be 535 agendas of directions in which we should be moving, or 535 directions in which we should try to stop things from moving.

That's why there have to be national priorities and therefore a sound basis for deciding on them. So how do we go about that?

One way is to sort the issues out as to which should be basically local issues and which should be federal or national. As the major example, we have a national consensus that control of education should be local. During the last presidential campaigns, it was jokingly noted that we were selecting a President of the United States, not a school superintendent. When studied carefully, President Bush's proposals on education dealt with only the 6 or 7% of the total spending on education that is done by the federal government. He was acknowledging that about 93 to 94% of the education spending is by the states and communities. His pledge was to further that local control, by sending the federal money to the local communities with less control but with at least expectations that they use that money so they get results with it. He was hopefully not indicating any intention to keep federalizing education. It can't be a major priority for a federal government that has so many other problems that really *are* federal.

The major one of those truly federal problems is of course national defense. That is our national government's first responsibility, regardless of whether we were interested in it during our last election or not.

Maybe the best way to determine our priorities is to see what our federal government does, as measured by what it spends in a year. Referring to the book, "The Budget of the U.S. Government for Fiscal 2001," we find that these were the major outlays (expenses) of the federal government for fiscal 1999, with Social Security included in these numbers (although we need to discuss that much more, as we get into this further): In millions of dollars:

TOTAL $1,703,040   100.0%
    Major Items:
       $ 390,041   22.9%   Social Security
           353,504   20.8%   Interest on the Public Debt
           274,873   16.1%   National Defense
           190,447   11.2%   Medicare
           108,042   6.3%   Medicaid

       $1,316,907   77.3%   Total of the Above

In other words, the federal government paid out one trillion 703 billion dollars in fiscal 1999 (including its payouts for all aspects of Social Security). Of that total, the biggest item was Social Security, which made up 22.9% of the 100.0%. To say it another way, out of every 4 or 5 dollars that the federal government paid out, 1 of those dollars was for Social Security.

Because of years and years of spending more money than it had (which we will also be discussing later), the federal government is borrowing so much money that the interest expense on that debt is 20.8% of this federal spending (when we count Social Security in the total). But it is essentially impossible to do much about this interest expense itself, other than indirectly, by either raising taxes, decreasing other spending, or both, until the debt can be brought down, *thereby* reducing this interest expense.

The third largest item in the federal budget is national defense, which has been the part of the budget that has been decreasing as a percentage of the total, but which is now at 16.1% of the total, or about 1 dollar in 6.

Medicare is next on the list, with spending at less than *half* the amount of Social Security. And Medicaid is the next largest item on the budget, accounting for about 6.3% of the total.

In just those 5 items, you have 77.3% of the federal budget. Focus on those, and you are dealing with the major outlays of the U.S. government.

That ranking of Social Security as the number one expense item in the federal budget argues strongly for moving it to the top of the agenda, *second only to national defense.*

This is certainly not to say that the other topics are not important. But it is to say that we need to focus on priorities, and not pick our agenda items based on polls or on a popularity contest, or on the basis of which topics are political "easy pickin's" or "hot potatoes." The choices have to be made on the basis of which topics are appropriately matters for the federal agenda and most important to our nation's future.

Number one is National Defense and number two is Social Security.

Once we have our priorities straight, we can move on to the subject of being sure that we are accurately defining the problem that we are setting out to solve.

Question #3

What Exactly *Is* the Problem??

When we set out to solve a problem, such as "Social Security," we need to be clear as to exactly what that problem *is*.

There are at least four things that we can say are *not* the problem we are trying to solve. We are not trying to figure out how to reduce current Social Security benefits. We are not trying to decide how to raise payroll taxes enough to pay for what Social Security is now promising. We are not trying to figure out how to "fix" Social Security. And we are not trying to decide how to "privatize" Social Security.

All of those are potentially *solutions* or part of some solution. But they are not the problem. We can't start off by working on *solutions*. First, we have to decide what it is that we are trying to do.

We could, on the one hand, make this an occasion to try to open up the subject of covering *all* of people's retirement income needs, and to "straighten *everything* out." A more modest approach would be simply to try to at least be sure we are able to continue to provide the present minimum level of retirement income, or to come as close as possible to that.

Right from the beginning, when Social Security was introduced back in the mid-1930's, it was never intended to provide *all* of a person's retirement income. Social Security was meant to provide only some sort of vaguely-defined "floor," some assurance that Americans wouldn't be left with no income at all when they reached their retirement years.

Over the years, this vague goal has come to be defined a bit more definitely as about 56% of what the Social Security Administration defines as "low earnings" (calculated in a very complicated manner, based on earnings in the later working years), or (as most often quoted) 42% of average earnings, and 34% of "high earnings."

We have to stop and acknowledge, though, that the trustees are also telling us that Social Security, as presently financed, is not going to be able to go on actually *paying* benefits at those levels. So we have to look at the possibility that it can't be a realistic goal to continue benefits at those levels.

We will need to do some hard thinking about what the Social Security problem, that we are trying to solve, really *is*.

But, for openers, this is a suggestion: the problem that we want to solve is:

"How can we best assure that our retirees continue to have a minimum retirement income equal to what Social Security presently provides, or at least as close as possible to that?"

There may be different ways to get there, but we need to start out with an agreement about what we are trying to accomplish, about where we are trying to go.

Question #4

Who Should Lead This Discussion and Make the Decisions?

There are actually a lot of answers to that question.

But to begin with, the President of the United States is the one person who must be *the* leader of this discussion of Social Security. The discussion is going to go nowhere until he personally leads it.

In recent years, we have watched an interesting little sideplay in which President Clinton held one of the two doors into the Social Security room and the Congressional leaders held the other door. Each one kept saying, "*You* go first!" and the other would insist that, "No, y*ou* go first." So no one went first. And that was because the Congressional leaders knew that they would be committing political suicide to try to take over the Presidential responsibilities, and the President knew that he wasn't yet ready to start proposing anything more than a very general approach of being responsible about Social Security financing.

President Bush knows that the President has to be the leader on this, and he has said that he will be. He has appointed a "bipartisan commission," but the danger of such groups is that they can become a substitute for decisive leadership.

"Bipartisan commissions" of maybe a dozen or more gurus or power figures have blue ribbons pinned on them and are supposed to go up on the mountain, cloister themselves, think great thoughts, and then come down from the hilltop and read to us from the tablets on which they have carved the answer. It isn't going to work.

This isn't *their* problem. It is *ours*. *We* are the "bipartisan commission" that should start out with at least 100 million members and hopefully still have at least 60 million members when we cross the decision-making finish line.

At a minimum, we have to learn from the disastrous experience of Hillary Clinton's closed door group that sought to give us all the answers on health care.

The decision has to be made by the nation, and that means that the nation itself must be taken, step by step, through the decision-making process, so we agree on what the problems are, how we are going to handle them, what the facts are, what our options are, and what decisions are best for all of us.

Our federal government needs to use the capacity that our nation has to communicate, through television, radio, the internet, the printed word and personal discussion. The President needs to use this capacity in new ways.

One way would be for him to personally lead the nation through this Social Security decision-making process by a series of televised addresses to the nation, taking the necessary questions in the order in which they need to be addressed.

Each address would be the introduction to a period of national discussion on only that part of the process. The President can then back that speech up by stumping the country, mainly to *educate* the nation about the facts. He can back his efforts by having a task force that is adequate to the follow-up task of seeing that this communication goes to every corner or category of the voting public. Polling can then measure whether the facts have been understood. If so, the nation is then ready for the next Presidential address and the next questions.

The candidates stump the nation to get themselves elected.

Why can't the President then do the same thing to advance one of the most important items on his agenda once he is in office?

Within the entertainment world, for example, a movie comes out and within about a week the whole nation has figured out whether they want to see it or whether it is a dud. Our ability to communicate with each other is phenomenal. The President needs to use the latest in our communication technology to lead us through the decision-making process on Social Security.

Beyond the conclusion, though, that the President of the United States has to be *the* leader of this discussion, we have to also agree that the task falls additionally on everyone who is an opinion leader for our country. That includes not only our politicians – at the federal, state and local level — but our media, our business and union leaders, our teachers, everyone right down to those who line up speakers for service club luncheons or assisted living discussion groups.

If the President can lead us to focus on these steps in an organized way, we should be able to astound ourselves with our capacity to reach consensus.

If we *can't* reach that consensus, on the other hand, then it follows that we aren't going to solve the problems.

After all, who *is* going to have to make these decisions?

Technically, the answer is, "269 top people in Washington, D.C." Those would be the President, at least 50 members of the Senate, and at least 218 members of the House of Representatives.

But that would be the bare minimum number, and really not a good decision if only that number of people made the decision.

The larger point, though, is that their only power is that they represent us.

They will never make this decision by themselves, or even be able to.

With about 280 million of us in the United States, of whom

around 200 million could be voters, we are going to have to have basic agreement or acceptance of the decisions by at least 60 million of us or it simply is not going to work. On something as important as Social Security, we aren't going to be able to live with any split decisions.

We are the ones who have to decide. We, not some little group of gurus, are going to have to be the jury and make the decision. To do that, we are going to have to listen to the case, gather a lot of information, absorb it, understand it, and then decide. It can't be done *for* us.

If we truly believe in the wisdom of the people and accordingly in the jury system in important matters, then it is the job of the President to present his case to the national jury. If he does, he will get a good decision.

So, assuming he does decide to present that case to us, what do we need to know in order to decide?

That's what comes next.

Question #5

What Should the "Code of Conduct" for Our Discussion Be?

At this particular time in our culture, we probably need to stop for a moment to agree on the way we are going to work together, the way we are going to treat each other, before we plunge into a discussion of something as important to all of us as Social Security.

In recent years, our society has made enormous economic progress. But at the same time, we have had a desecration of those standards that we as a people want in our public communication and our political leadership.

We now have a society that unfortunately understands what the phrase "the politics of personal destruction" means. We have repeatedly watched the lives of public figures be trashed. We expect "spin," instead of truth, from our senators and representatives, and rank them respectively 17th and 23rd out of 32 professions, when rating them for their honesty and ethics. We have gone through a presidential impeachment, learned the slippery meaning of "is," and polarized our thinking about our politicians.

Then within this last year we have polarized our society even further by getting into a major conflict over what "a vote" means. There is a lot of lingering animosity, even a search for further opportunities to stir anger, to get everyone fired up, to look for winners and losers, to find a good fight.

This is not a good atmosphere in which to jump into a discussion of Social Security. We need to acknowledge that maybe the quality of our national discourse right now leaves a bit to be desired. In sports terms, before we start the next season, we all need to review the rules and be sure that we agree that it is best for all of us to get back to following them. We shouldn't start the next "game" until we are all committed to again being civil, positive and responsible.

That's a good generality, but we need to be more specific than that. As we discuss Social Security, as our opinion leaders appear in public and on TV, as representatives of the many "special" interests of our country testify before committees of Congress, as members of Congress speak, as our many "commentators" comment, as our media work as the go-betweens bringing much of the information to us, we need to be constantly aware of the quality of our communication.

Each one of us, in short, needs to be a referee, calling it "out of bounds" when our rules are being violated. The discussion of Social Security is so important to all of us that we can't let it turn into a free-for-all.

So we need to agree that we will proceed...

...one step at a time, skipping no steps in this decision-making process. We all need to be involved, and there is much that we have to agree on and learn before we can ever get far enough down the road that we are ready to begin making the decisions. We can't be jumping to conclusions. We can't have good opinions if we really don't yet even know what we are talking about. We need to take it step by step, making sure at various checkpoints along the road in this journey that we are all still together, and not leaving too many behind.

...honestly, particularly in our use of words. Words are the main way we exchange facts and ideas, and politicians seem to be able to stretch the meaning of words the most. As we'll be covering, most of the main words that we use in discussing Social Security financing are at the least misleading, and at the worst actually downright lies. We have to demand utmost honesty, which will frankly be a big change. We will have to *keep* demanding it, because the dishonest vocabulary has become a bad habit that leads us to bad decisions.

...seriously, soberly and with loving concern for all.
One simple but enduring guideline can be that we "do unto others as you would have them do unto you." Some of the more religious among us may want to think in terms of, "Not my will, but Thy will be done."

Throughout our country (and the world, for that matter), we are family first. We are sons and daughters, mothers and fathers, grandparents and great grandparents first. We love and care for each other the most in our families. The children care for their grandparents, the grandparents care about their grandchildren, and the older we get, the more we know that what really counts in life is not all the "stuff," but these relationships. What we are most proud of is in a family picture.

Yes, we are parts of groups at work or in our social life, but those associations are secondary. So when we start classifying each other by our associations, all of us need to remember that our first and most meaningful associations are with each other as family and friends, as people who truly care about each other.

The young *do* care about the old. The old *do* care about the young. As good human beings, we *do* care about each other, and that goodness can come out when we work out answers that *are* best for all of us.

...with constant attention to "fairness, not favoritism." We will of course all need to speak up for and represent our own self interests. But one particular feature of national politics is that those who want to get the most out of Washington for themselves are therefore those who spend the most time there, pushing their own self interests before Congress. It can turn into all "me" and "mine." The Congressional committees may hear little, if anything, from those who have to actually *pay* for some of these things.

It's a distortion in the process that we have to watch out for. All of us have to know that our senators and representatives are hearing from us, too, and that they are devoted to fairness for *all* of us, not favoritism for the few who speak the most and the loudest, or have the most money.

...with a clear understanding that those who wish to create or capitalize on personal conflict are not welcome in this discussion. We have had our fill of character assassination, of efforts to destroy people personally because someone disagrees with their ideas. We want the media to "put the hook on" those few who specialize in trashmouthing, in going for the jugular, in looking for the conflicts that can stir the viewer ratings, and to do us all a favor by pulling these people off the stage.

We don't want Social Security to be cast as a fight, a battle, another political "war against...," a conflict of people, generations, political parties or "the rich" vs. "the poor." To the contrary, we need an atmosphere in which we all endeavor to learn as much as we can, not only about the facts but about each other's needs. We need to focus on the problems, the facts, and the right answers, not on fighting with or tearing down each other as people.

We will need less incendiary language, less labeling, less

name-calling. If people start calling proposed solutions "risky schemes," it needs to be in the context that just about anything that will solve the problems –regardless of what it is—will be risky. But it won't be a "scheme." It's also unlikely that any of the proposed solutions to the problems of Social Security will be "a sinister plot." We need to be sure that words are not being lobbed into the Social Security discussion like grenades.

We will need less talk that stirs up emotions, foments anger, creates distrust and scares people. Instead, we will need words that assure people with the facts.

It would be nice if we didn't even have to stop and say that, but we *do* need to. Social Security is too important a topic.

...by accepting responsibility, rather than claiming status as victims. Social Security is such a big problem that it is very unlikely that we will solve it without every one of us having to give up something. We will each need to contribute our part to the solution. Quite simply, we need to accept the idea that we can't claim that we are victims, "not responsible for this," so we find a way to pass the buck to others, to give them the bill.

It's fine and dandy to proclaim, "Something has to be *done!*" That fails to clarify who it is that is supposed to be doing the doing. If something indeed does have to be done, then all of us have to decide what part we will take responsibility for.

At some point in sorting all of these Social Security problems out, it may get down to the point where you are, in effect, at the table, and someone says, "We all came to the party and had a good time. Now we all have to pay the bill." That could be a difficult moment, defining for each of us whether we are going to accept responsibility and do our part.

As a people, Americans face and accept responsibility when they understand it.

So our first job has to be to understand the problems of Social Security and then to ask, "What can I do to help?"

...without stereotypes and assumptions that are probably wrong. We are not thinking clearly when we assume that, because someone belongs to a group we can predict how that person thinks. Because some people are over 50 years old and like the magazine and discount programs of AARP does not mean that they are in one political party or the other, have closed minds on Social Security, think only of protecting their own interests, don't care about their children, grandchildren and great grandchildren, and wouldn't support significant change in Social Security if it were for the good of all.

Similar reasoning applies to those who are members of chambers of commerce, unions of teachers or the trades, or of political parties.

We devalue people if we think of them as so beholden to various groups that we no longer give them credit for thinking as individuals, as people with minds of their own and with the capacities to make their own decisions.

...without making (the African-American) race a divisive issue. The "race card" has been overplayed, and has no place in the Social Security discussion. In truth, African-Americans may get the short end of the stick in the present Social Security system, mainly because of their typically shorter life spans (and therefore less years in which they receive retirement benefits). But if we choose as a nation to have this dialogue about Social Security, it is because we are seeking to come up with the best answers for *everyone.* Let's not turn it into an issue of color of skin, because it isn't. Racial demagoguery isn't welcome, and would poison the well rather than helping us work things out.

...without turning this into matters for the courts and lawyers. After O.J. Simpson, impeachment and Florida, some of us might be anticipating that Social Security will soon become a class action suit of one generation versus the other. That is the last thing we need.

The major part of our job is going to be not to fight, but to learn. If someone starts wanting to bring the lawyers into this process, we are way off track and need to get back to communicating and cooperating.

...remembering the effects of inflation. This is worth mentioning, because we will be talking about dollars now and dollars many years in the future, and those are not the same dollars.

For example, if we have inflation of about 3% per year, today's dollar will be worth 50 cents (in today's spending power) in about 24 years. With "normal" inflation of around 3%, in other words, it will take twice as many dollars 24 years from now to pay for the same thing.

We're going to be talking about whole life spans, so that will mean 25, 50 and 75 years from now. Several hundred thousand dollars may sound like a lot of money 40 years from now, but we need to keep "current" dollars in mind, those being future dollars that won't buy as much as a dollar will today.

It is very important to all of us that inflation be kept low. Otherwise, it is difficult to save for the future. Anything that we save keeps going down in value, to the extent that we have inflation. One of the rules of the game has to always be concern about the control of inflation.

...with full participation, not apathy. Maybe it is to some degree a matter of available time, but the record seems to be that the seniors have time to stay informed and to vote, but that the younger generations are currently politically apathetic.

In the 1996 presidential elections, around two thirds of those age 55-74 voted, but less than 30% of those 18-24. An American Express Young Voter Poll, published less than one month before the 2000 presidential election said that one third of those 16-21 years old didn't know who the presidential candidates were and three-fourths of them didn't know the vice-presidential candidate for either major party. But, as one columnist noted, "Fortunately, the election is multiple choice!"

One possible explanation for this political indifference among the young is that no generation has ever had it so good. So why worry? The problem, though, is that Social Security is something they really had better start not only thinking about, but worrying about. They are paying for it, the price is going to start escalating soon, and Social Security may well crash before they retire.

This discussion of Social Security is a wonderful opportunity for the younger folks to get involved in "politics," which is, after all, our working together on problems that affect all of us. But if, at the worst, the younger generation stays indifferent, wiser heads are going to have to represent them in this debate and look out for them, because there may be a lot of people looking for someone else to pay the bill.

...by saving our opinions and conclusions until we understand the facts. When we are asked what we think about some issue, it is hard to admit, "I really don't know enough about it to even have an intelligent opinion on that subject." Yet that is probably what almost all of us should answer when asked what our opinions are about Social Security.

Social Security is complex, we have been misinformed about it in large part, and those who say they know the answers are probably also those who would tell you, "Don't confuse me with the facts."

We all have a lot of homework to do before we are ready for the test.

...with polling to verify knowledge and understanding, more than opinions. Polling can be very valuable as a measurement of whether we, as a nation, have our facts straight and are making our way through the necessary steps enroute to final decision-making. But to be using polls to figure out what our uneducated opinions or premature conclusions are is a waste of time and a distraction from the learning process that we should be working on.

...with more fear of <u>in</u>action than fear of action. We are not going to solve the problems of Social Security if we are afraid to make big changes and do bold things. If we are controlled by fear, which is a very important emotion for politicians, our objective will become to relieve or avoid our fears, rather than to solve the problems.

But the greatest danger is that, by responding more to our fears than to our faith, we will fail to do enough to really *solve* the problems. Unfortunately, that is what we have done with Social Security every time it became a crisis in the past.

We see fear at work already, as various politicians float the idea that maybe some workers should be allowed to invest 2% of their pay in private accounts. As a matter of fact, 2% isn't enough money to solve anything at all. But the 2% idea is being floated because of the fear that the public can't at this point accept any higher percentage. No, the politicians know 2% is not a real solution. But they are afraid to try for more. That's the kind of thinking we need to get past, mainly by learning the facts and then facing up to them.

... with the courage to face up to the costs of what we want. The first conclusion in politics is usually that once you give government benefits to people, or tell them they will get them, you can never take them away. Or, if you do manage to take any benefits away, it had better be pretty sneaky and people had better not figure out what is going on.

The matter of fact is that our federal politicians have a very consistent record of being unable to face up to the cost of what they do for us. That is because they reflect the thinking of those who put them in office. We want the goodies, but we want someone else to pay the bill. Government is the very means by which some of us want that redistribution to be carried out.

The real problem for the politicians happens when all of the promises are getting so far out of hand that there is nowhere left to tax or borrow in order to, in so many words, keep the party going. No politician wants to be the one who goes to his or her constituents and has to tell them, "Not only is the party over, but *your* party is over." That's not what being a politician is supposed to be about.

As we work our way toward the decision-making phase of the Social Security discussion, it is going to start to become clear that there is an enormous bill to be paid, and that *somebody* is actually going to have to *pay* it! Oh horrible real world. No rose garden after all.

We will be getting into discussion of the various options as to who pays what. But before we even get to that point in the discussion, we need to acknowledge that the most cowardly decision of all would be if we pass the bill along, not only to our children, but to *their* children, too. Why would we even think of doing that? Why? Because those children haven't been born yet, we can run up the bill and pass it on to them and they aren't here yet to defend themselves and object.

...with a commitment to really <u>solve</u> the problems!

If we are going to go through this whole subject with this much care, giving it this much time, we can't come up short and fail to really take those actions that <u>solve</u> the problems.

We may well reach that point at which our political representatives in Washington, knowing the pulse of the nation, conclude that they are now in agreement. But it may also be necessary for someone to then say, "Fine. We're all agreed on what to do. The only hitch is that it doesn't really solve the problems. So we have to keep working at it. We're not through yet."

That will probably be the moment when we find out who is realistic and courageous, and who really is unwilling to be.

But it will be easier for our politicians to do what needs to be done, if we make it clear to them that *we* are willing to be realistic and courageous, so they are not going out on a limb but are in fact representing *us*.

The bottom line is that we ourselves are the ones who, at the moment of decision, will need to be informed, realistic and courageous.

Add your own choices of ways in which we can proceed. Or object to some of the above ways. But we *do* need to agree on a code of conduct for our discussion of Social Security. We may disagree on all of the various *ways* in which we might do it, but we do need to reach a consensus about being civil.

If we are going to discuss Social Security and bring the nation to a well-informed point of decision-making, we will need to do it with respect. Respect for not only the importance of the subject but for each other.

We need to stop long enough to make a commitment to each other that such respect will be our way of working together. Only when we have made that commitment are we then ready to move on to the next step.

When we're ready, the next step is to start learning all the facts that we have to understand before we are really ready to move toward decision-making.

Question #6

What Are the Facts about the Federal Budget?

Rather than wading right into a bunch of accounting, let's start with a little myth, a make-believe story about Mary and Harry.

Although Mary and Harry both have bankers who work *very* closely together, and this sometimes confuses people, Mary and Harry each run a separate company. Mary runs "Mary Retirement" and Harry runs "Harry Subsidies."

Some people call the two companies simply "Get Your Goodies Later" (Mary) and "Get Your Goodies Now" (Harry). Others say, "You pay for your ticket now, and go to the party later" in Mary's company, whereas in Harry Subsidies the saying seems to be, "Whoever's paying for it, the party is going on right now."

But Mary and Harry actually do have two very different companies, even if to a large degree they serve the same customers. Mary runs "The Big Retirement Company" and Harry runs "The Everything-BUT-the-Big-Retirement Company."

Each of them runs a regular company, financially. Each company has its money coming in (its revenue, its income), its money going out (its bills, its spending, its expenses) and then ends up each year either with some money left over or short of money. If, for example, Mary pays all her bills and still has some left in the bank, she lends it out, charges interest to those who borrow the money, and then has more money ("interest income") to put into her bank. And if Harry tries to pay all his bills and comes up short, he goes out and borrows what he needs, pays for it ("interest expense") and records it on his books as an increase in his expenses.

Both Mary and Harry are good at public relations and at developing their images in their customers' eyes. Mary, for example, has her customers convinced that they are making "contributions" (instead of paying "payroll taxes"), something like "premiums," because they think they are buying "insurance" and thereby becoming "guaranteed" to future payouts in direct relationship to their contributions. As one of her customers put it, "It's kind of like life insurance, where you pay for a long time and then they pay <u>someone else</u> when you <u>die.</u> But with Mary's company, you pay for a long time and then they pay <u>you</u> when you <u>live</u> (that long)!"

Harry, on the other hand, gets his customers to think of it as belonging to a "Union," to which they pay dues (not "income taxes"). He provides his customers with all sorts of subsidies, not many years later in their life, but right now. The major examples are that he sees that they are protected from other unions, pays a lot of their medical bills, and passes out special payments to all his friends. Like, he pays the farmers (wheat, cotton, peanut, tobacco, dairy, sugar, etc.) to follow his rules and keep their prices up. He gives special deals to people who own homes, to girls who have babies without fathers or educations, to those who claim victimhood instead of responsibility, to enormous companies who want marketing help, to less than 1% of all the small businesses in the country, to local schools, — really, to anyone who can convince him or enough of the 535 members of his two boards of directors that they have special interests that need more money than other people can get.

So basically he is in the business of passing out goodies right now, while making sure that his members remain unaware of, or ignore or escape the bill.

The other side of his business is that he does have to pay for all of this somehow, so he does have an agreement with his members that about half of them won't pay any dues *at all*, 5% of his members pay over half of the dues, and in fact just 1% of his members pay about a third of all the dues. It's an easy system to keep going, as long as he can keep class warfare alive ("the rich," the "robber barons," "Wall Streeters," etc.), and get the majority of his members to vote to have the dues paid by the minority. In fact, he sometimes thinks of his members as either the "givers" (those who pay dues, and who don't want to, and think they could get more services from that money themselves) or the "takers" (who don't pay dues, but want to get more goodies). And, as he often says (slightly changing what George Bernard Shaw said), "The company that robs Peter to pay Paul can always count on Paul's support!"

But Harry Subsidies has been having troubles making ends meet. In fact, the company has been losing money every one of the last 42 years (from 1958 through 1999) . By "losing money," we mean paying out more than it is taking in. Well, let's correct that statement. One year (1960), the company actually had $6.23 left over (after paying its bills) out of every $1,000 that it took in. But they made up for that quickly: the next year the company spent $1,045.77 for every $1,000 it took in. Mistakes will happen. And one other year (1999), the company managed to claim that it was "in the black" by holding some bills to pay in the year 2000. That way they could say they spent only $999.48 of every $1,000.00 they took in.

To be honest about it, Harry Subsidies has had a *really* hard time paying its bills. One year, his main message to the members was that "the era of big Unions is over," even though he took in *twice* as much in dues in 1998 as his company did just ten years before, in 1988. And in the early 1990's, before he ran head on into a change of his board of directors, Harry Subsidies was regularly spending between $1,360 to $1,430 for every $1,000 of dues that it was collecting. It averaged out as spending of $300 billion more than he had *every year* (this being a BIG company). In corporate lingo, he was running Harry Subsidies at an annual loss equal to 36% to 43% of revenues, heading to what would be, for other companies, immediate bankruptcy. And in early 1994, Harry submitted his annual budget to the board of directors, showing his plan to spend about a quarter of a trillion dollars *each year* in excess of his revenues for the next five years (1995 through 1999), that being typically about 23% more than what he was taking in.

Harry was definitely perpetually in need of money to cover his bills. But he had two ways of handling the problem, one being to simply go out and borrow money from the members, actually pay them (interest) for the use of their money (even though it ran his expenses up even higher), but of course to use it to pay bills. The second of the two ways was a little slight of hand that had started being very handy in about 1985, and which was getting more useful every year. In fact, it had in about the last 10 years gone from being the source of around $50 billion of cash to pay bills each year, to now being a source for over $100 billion a year, and headed toward being a source for $200 billion a year!

But it wasn't a source that either he or the members of the board of directors really wanted the Union to know much about, particularly when those board members were out dishing out more and more goodies to the members and didn't want to deny the members anything and *certainly* didn't want to tell them that the Union couldn't pay its bills.

And at his annual State of the Union speech covering 1999,

What Are the Facts about the Federal Budget? 53

Harry made sure he got *lots* of credit for getting Harry Subsidies back into the black. Harry told them the Union had come up with its first "surplus" in years: $124 billion!

Mary, meanwhile, though, was doing better financially. Mainly, it was because she had ticket prices that required people to pay more each year than she was actually paying out that year, so she could build up money in the bank. A few years back, she had studied her business and had been advised that she was going to have a *lot* more people "going to the party" in a few years, the party was getting to cost much more per year, and so she had better build up even *more* in the bank account to be ready. So she started charging her higher income customers more and more each year, (although it didn't change what benefits they would get at the party).

And so her bank account was *really* growing! By 1999, she was able to bank nearly 40% more than she paid out; in other words, of every $1400 that she took in, she paid out $1000 and put $400 in the bank. By 2003, it would be up to more than $500 going into her bank account for every $1000 she paid out, and by 2005, $550! And her forecast was that she would be able to keep doing that until at least 2010, not even counting the interest income that she was apparently also able to put in the bank by loaning this extra money out until she needed it.

But rumors had started about "troubles" of some sort with her guaranteed parties, and she had had to continually emphasize that, from everything that her experts could guess, there was no problem until the year 2037. The press repeated this information for her continually. So, for example, someone who was 50 years old in 2001 would do this arithmetic: "I'm 50, there's no problem until 36 years from now in 2037, I probably won't even be around by then, so why worry?" This same person (getting close to the party, and speaking too for those already at the party) did, however, let everyone know regularly that he did not want "his boat rocked" in the least in *his* lifetime,

So Mary generally kept this 50-and-over group pacified and assured that no one was going to break up their party. Next, fortunately, the under-50 crowd seemed to be either apathetic or willing to keep paying for tickets but not really expecting to ever make it to the party. And, interestingly, Mary didn't even have to deal with a third group at all: those who hadn't been born yet. They were going to be born into a system that would, for example, charge someone born in 2001 for tickets, with his payments starting probably around 2018 and helping the party keep going to at least 2037, although his tickets wouldn't be good for anything until at least 2066.

So there was lots of money in Mary's account at the Trust Fund Bank (in fact, in the hundreds of billions of dollars, headed into the *trillions*), the party was going strong, and everyone in Mary's company was either happy or not complaining.

One thing Mary had said once to Harry was that if anything really got their customers excited, it was SEX, so it should damned sure never come out in public that they were really, financially, so to speak, "sleeping together."

But one day there was an "audit," where some outside accountants came into Harry Subsidies and wanted to examine the Union's accounting books. They wanted to see where the money was coming from and where it was going. What they found got them upset enough that they also went over and checked Mary's books. Sure enough, it was all true.

There was no money in Mary's Trust Fund Bank account. She had loaned it all to Harry and he had spent every penny of it. All that was in Mary's bank account at the Trust Fund Bank was either a pile of IOUs from Harry for what she had been loaning him for years, or bills that she had sent him for the interest she was charging him, on which bills he had written, "Put it on my tab." She had been recording these all as "interest in-

What Are the Facts about the Federal Budget? 55

come" for her Trust Fund Bank account.

The auditors found out, for example, that when Harry had said Harry Subsidies' budget had been in the black by $124 billion in 1999, the books actually showed that the Union *itself* had been less than $1 billion in the black ("On Budget") but had borrowed $124 billion from Mary, slipped it into its financial statements as "income" ("Off Budget"), and then called the total "THE Budget."

The auditors asked Mary how she could lend money, so *much* money, in fact every spare cent she had, to Harry, when she *knew* that he hadn't been able to pay his own bills for the last 40 years, let alone pay back any loans from her. She said he had guaranteed her that he would pay her back when she needed it. He had said nothing about "…if he could."

The auditors pointed out that she was going to need him to start paying her back in about ten years, and asked how he was going to be able to do it. He said he would have basically only two ways: to tell his Union members that they had to take a cut in benefits (which he knew they wouldn't do) or else raise their dues. (Or, he noted that as a variation on raising dues, he could borrow some more money from them and then stall off the date of paying them back until he *could* raise their dues).

Then the word started getting out at Mary's party that, without all of those hundreds of billions of dollars that were supposed to be in the Trust Fund Bank, but weren't, the talk about having the party last until 2037 was just talk. The party might have to start winding down around 2010, unless Mary could get Harry to raise dues enough to pay her back.

But Harry knew how to handle a potential crisis, his Union members *and* Mary's customers. When told he might lose his job in the biggest sexual/financial scandal in his Union's history, he said, "We'll just have to win, then." And so far, he has.

For one thing, he pointed out that he was not in this alone, by any means. Mary and all her officers and "trustees" knew all about it. And so did all 535 members of Harry's two boards. But none of them had wanted to "rock the boat" enough to really break up the party, so they had all played along with it too. And as long as Harry kept saying "surplus" and Mary kept saying "2037," no one seemed to care about the details or whatever this "stuff" was that the auditors had found.

Harry also made the point that he didn't take the money and spend it on himself. He spent it on the members of his Union, so you could say that they got their money back, one way or another. They just got it earlier than they expected. They had thought the money would be used for the parties put on by Mary Retirement, but instead it had been spent on other goodies that the Union members wanted right now and couldn't have paid for otherwise.

Most of Mary's customers were, as we mentioned, also in Harry's Union. He liked to refer to his Union members as "the troops," probably because they fell into line when he needed them to and didn't ask a lot of questions. The last time Harry was seen, he had just told a reporter, "Not to worry! The party is going strong, and I'm out of here! It's somebody else's turn." Then he went out to lead the troops once more in chanting, "Save Mary Retirement! Save Mary Retirement!" They loved it.

No one seemed to care that the auditors were claiming that Harry had ripped off Mary's bank account for nearly $600 billion in the last 8 years.

The main trouble with the little "Mary and Harry" story, of course, is that it isn't just a story. It is an attempt to give you some idea of how our federal government keeps us confused about what is going on. They do it by mixing the Social Security accounting in with the accounting of the rest of the government.

Everything would be much clearer all around if the accounting for these two separate operations or businesses was also kept separate. But let's at least run through a little history of how it all got put together and of how there have been efforts ever since to get it separated again.

In the late 1960's, President Lyndon Johnson brought the reporting of all of the income and outgo of the federal government, including Social Security, into one big "unified" or "consolidated" budget. This became "*the*" budget, and we thereafter had "*the*" surplus or *"the"* deficit.

The major problem in this "consolidation" was that it put together two entirely different businesses. Social Security was trying to plan ahead for projected future needs and collect money and set it aside until it was needed in future years. This meant that "surpluses" in *current* years might be entirely inadequate, because they weren't setting aside enough money for expected *future* needs. But the rest of the government was looking at its here-and-now, current year results.

What of course soon became apparent was that by totaling the results of these two dissimilar businesses, Social Security could have a big "surplus" (that might really be too small for what it knew its future needs to be), the rest of the government could spend more than it was taking in and therefore be running a *deficit* in *its* business, but all of this got covered up by making it one big total that showed that, in net, "*the*" budget had a "surplus."

So Congress began making efforts to get Social Security back *out* of the budget. But these efforts really put Congress at cross-purposes, because having Social Security *in* the budget made it easier for Congress to spend far in excess of its real income and to use Social Security to cover it all up.

The Social Security Amendments of 1983 required that beginning with the federal budget for fiscal 1993 (ten years later, in other words), income and expenditures for Social Security (OASI, DI, and HI) would be excluded from the totals of the budget put together by the President and Congress.

By 1985, The Balanced Budget and Emergency Deficit Control Act said that, among other things, 1993 was too long to wait to get Social Security "off budget," and that it should happen in 1986. You might have thought it was clear and that it would happen in 1986. But it didn't.

So the Omnibus Budget Reconciliation Act of 1990 again clarified that the income and outgo of the Social Security funds were to be removed from all of the calculations of the federal budget, including the budget deficit or surplus. Social Security was "not to be included in the budget totals themselves." Pretty clear. But it still didn't really happen.

However, on August 15, 1994, President Clinton did sign into law the Social Security Independence and Program Improvements Act of 1994, establishing the Social Security Administration as an "independent" agency, effective March 31, 1995. This at least took the Social Security Administration out of Health and Human Services. (And the Social Security Administration is also separated at least physically from Washington, D.C. by being in Baltimore, Maryland.)

But to skip forward to President Clinton's book, "The Budget of the United States Government, Fiscal Year 2001," submitted to Congress in February, 2000, you will find the typical annual explanation:

"Though social security and the Postal Service are now off-budget, they continue to be Federal programs. Indeed, social security currently accounts for about one-fourth of all Federal spending. Hence, the budget documents include these funds and focus on the Federal totals that combine the on-budget and off-budget amounts."

In other words, "The law told us to take it 'off-budget,' but since it is so big, we are going to put it back in and continue to

What Are the Facts about the Federal Budget?

show it as part of 'the' budget." And they might have added, "...because that enables us to keep you confused, so we can go on spending the Social Security surplus."

The result is that the President submits "his budget" and everyone goes right on talking about "the budget," with Social Security of course still in it, and the press goes right along with this and maintains the public understanding that there is only one budget with one surplus or deficit.

An example of how badly this can confuse everything was the situation, just a few years ago, where the nation came within one vote in the Senate of having a "Balanced Budget Amendment" proposed to the Constitution, of course with Social Security right back in there and included as part of the budget, with its surpluses used to cover the hanky-panky in the rest of the government.

The accounting has kept the public totally confused. So let's wade into the numbers and see if we can make clear what is going on, not in "the" budget that they like to talk about in Washington, but in the two separate budgets:

"Off-budget," which is Social Security's retirement and disability income plans (OASI + DI), but not Medicare

"On-budget," which is everything else and which does include Medicare.

Separating "off-budget" from "on-budget"

Happily, the annual budget books *do* summarize, on one page, those two separate categories, showing for each one its own income, its own outgo, and its own surplus or deficit. An excerpt from these "Historical Tables" from the Fiscal Year 2000 Budget is shown as Table 6-1 on page 60.

TABLE 6-1: Summary of Receipts, Outlays and Surpluses or Deficits, 1980-1999 actual and 2000-2005 estimate, shown in Total, as On-Budget, and as Off-Budget ("Off-Budget" being Social Security)

THE BUDGET FOR FISCAL YEAR 2001, HISTORICAL TABLES

SUMMARY OF RECEIPTS, OUTLAYS, AND SURPLUSES OR DEFICITS(−)

(in millions of dollars)

Year	Total Receipts	Total Outlays	Total Surplus or Deficit (−)	On-Budget Receipts	On-Budget Outlays	On-Budget Surplus or Deficit (−)	Off-Budget Receipts	Off-Budget Outlays	Off-Budget Surplus or Deficit (−)	Medicare Solvency
1980	517,112	590,947	−73,835	403,903	476,618	−72,715	113,209	114,329	−1,120	
1981	599,272	678,249	−78,976	469,097	543,053	−73,956	130,176	135,196	−5,020	
1982	617,766	745,755	−127,989	474,299	594,351	−120,052	143,467	151,404	−7,937	
1983	600,562	808,385	−207,822	453,242	661,277	−208,035	147,320	147,108	212	
1984	666,486	851,874	−185,388	500,411	686,061	−185,650	166,075	165,813	262	
1985	734,088	946,423	−212,334	547,918	769,615	−221,698	186,171	176,807	9,363	
1986	769,215	990,460	−221,245	568,986	806,962	−237,976	200,228	183,498	16,731	
1987	854,353	1,004,122	−149,769	640,951	810,290	−169,339	213,402	193,832	19,570	
1988	909,303	1,064,489	−155,187	667,812	861,798	−193,986	241,491	202,691	38,800	
1989	991,190	1,143,671	−152,481	727,525	932,760	−205,235	263,666	210,911	52,754	
1990	1,031,969	1,253,198	−221,229	750,314	1,028,133	−277,819	281,656	225,065	56,590	
1991	1,055,041	1,324,403	−269,361	761,157	1,082,716	−321,559	293,885	241,687	52,198	
1992	1,091,279	1,381,684	−290,404	788,853	1,129,345	−340,492	302,426	252,339	50,087	
1993	1,154,401	1,409,512	−255,110	842,467	1,142,925	−300,457	311,934	266,587	45,347	
1994	1,258,627	1,461,902	−203,275	923,601	1,182,530	−258,929	335,026	279,372	55,654	
1995	1,351,830	1,515,837	−164,007	1,000,751	1,227,173	−226,422	351,079	288,664	62,415	
1996	1,453,062	1,560,572	−107,510	1,085,570	1,259,668	−174,098	367,492	300,904	66,588	
1997	1,579,292	1,601,282	−21,990	1,187,302	1,290,656	−103,354	391,990	310,626	81,364	
1998	1,721,798	1,652,611	69,187	1,305,999	1,336,007	−30,008	415,799	316,604	99,195	
1999	1,827,454	1,703,040	124,414	1,382,986	1,382,262	724	444,468	320,778	123,690	
2000 estimate	1,956,252	1,789,562	166,690	1,479,489	1,460,633	18,856	476,763	328,929	147,834	
2001 estimate	2,019,031	1,835,033	183,998	1,519,136	1,494,777	24,359	499,895	340,256	159,639	
2002 estimate	2,061,220	1,895,317	185,903	1,558,994	1,545,153	13,841	522,226	350,164	172,062	15,400
2003 estimate	2,147,489	1,962,853	184,636	1,603,242	1,602,924	318	544,247	359,929	184,318	12,600
2004 estimate	2,236,091	2,041,131	194,960	1,669,431	1,669,089	342	566,660	372,042	194,618	
2005 estimate	2,340,896	2,125,451	215,445	1,742,330	1,740,539	1,791	598,566	384,912	213,654	

Source: Page 20, The Budget of the United States Government for Fiscal Year 2001, Historical Tables, U.S. Government Printing Office

The surplus in "the" budget

First, look at the third column from the left, "Total, Surplus or Deficit(-)." In this column, you see the total of both Social Security and everything else. This is what the President presents as "the" (unified or consolidated) budget. We happily go from big deficits to having a "surplus" starting in the year 1998 and then having it get bigger every year, heading toward a "surplus" of more than $200 billion in the year 2005.

This is "the surplus" that the politicians are scrambling to spend, or out of which to give tax cuts, or allocating among spending, tax cuts, reduction of the debt or "saving Social Security." This is the total that <u>in</u>cludes Social Security.

This is the column the President and Congress look at when they crow about having "balanced the budget."

The Social Security surplus

Now look in the "Off-Budget, Surplus or Deficit (-)" column, over at the right. This column tells you that Social Security (which is what "Off-Budget" means) has had more income than expense, starting in 1983.

In fact, that surplus, that amount of cash not being paid out by Social Security each year, is up to more than $123 billion in the year 1999 and is expected to be over *$200 billion* in the year 2005. Look at that column carefully and be sure you understand that. Very important, because those surpluses are expected to go right on increasing, so that they are bigger every year for the next 15 years and will still be over $200 billion per year 20 years from now.

If you start adding up all of these annual surpluses in the Social Security accounts, you can (1) understand how these

Social Security surpluses have already added up to nearly a trillion dollars through the year 2000, (2) see that these *Social Security* surpluses are expected to be nearly *another* trillion in the five years 2001 through 2005, and (3) begin to see, as these annual surpluses continue to grow *in the Social Security fund*, how these surpluses are forecasted to accumulate to create a balance of over *$6 trillion* dollars by the early 2020's.

(That is, if the money isn't spent on other things by then, but we'll get to that).

Now, the "on-budget" surplus, that being for everything other than Social Security

However, now look at the column toward the middle of the page, "On-Budget, Surplus or Deficit (-)." Here you start to get at the truth of the matter. This is the column that tells you *really* what the government is doing with its own budget, if the politicians were actually willing to take Social Security out of the totals.

For example, let's look at this "On-Budget" (that is, the actual income and outgo of our government, with Social Security –with the retirement trust — left out of the budget, left out of the totals) for only the years 1990 through 1994 (after which time there was a little change in Congress). We are looking here at "the company," "the business itself," leaving out the separate matter of how the retirement trust fund is doing.

This is an extract of the "On-Budget" numbers for those years, with an additional column added to show what the deficit was, as a percentage of Receipts (or, in other words, as a percentage of Income):

What Are the Facts about the Federal Budget?   63

"IF WE CAN SPEND A DEFICIT, WE CAN SURE AS HELL SPEND A SURPLUS."

THE WASHINGTON TIMES

Copyright © 2000 News World Communications, Inc. Reprinted with permission of The Washington Times.

Govt Fiscal Year	Receipts	Outlays	Deficit	% Deficit
(in millions of dollars per year):				
1990	$750,314	$1,028,133	$277,819	-37.0%
1991	761,157	1,082,716	321,559	-42.2%
1992	788,853	1,129,345	340,492	-43.2%
1993	842,467	1,142,925	300,457	-35.7%
1994	923,601	1,182,530	258,929	-28.0%

In those five years, our government, ("on budget," meaning, not counting Social Security) ran up deficits totaling $1 trillion 500 billion. In just five years.

For every $1.00 of receipts coming in each year, our government spent somewhere between $1.28 and $1.43. If we did that in our personal lives or in our businesses, we would be bankrupt. But the odds are very strong that you had no idea that this was going on.

Now go back to that same column in the excerpt from the 2001 Budget book, "On-Budget, Surplus or Deficit (-)" and track down to the years 1999 and thereafter.

In fiscal 1999, for the first time in decades, the budget of the government (again, leaving Social Security out of it, in this calculation) actually showed a "surplus" *of its own!* It amounted to $724 million on income of $1,382,986,000,000 (or nearly $1 trillion 400 billion). That is a "surplus" of about *one twentieth of one percent*, and as a matter of fact that so-called "surplus" was created on the books in large part by pushing the accounting for expenses forward into the next year. So it was essentially a phony surplus.

Now you can see in the same column that President Clinton has estimated that in the 5 years, 2001 through 2005, the government will spend more every year, and will for those 5 years in total still run a total surplus of $40 billion 651 million, which amounts to a surplus for those five years of less than one half of one percent. Don't place any bets on it. The assumptions supporting that forecast are in fact a joke. And those assumptions did not include a big tax cut.

The reason that you should definitely not count on this *real* surplus developing in the actual (non-Social-Security) operations of our government is that the politicians don't want us to know or even think about this column. They want us all to focus on that "Total" surplus, over to the left, roaring on up toward

What Are the Facts about the Federal Budget?

> MY COLLEAGUE CAN BETTER EXPLAIN THE ECONOMIC ASSUMPTIONS ON WHICH THE BUDGET IS BASED.

Copyright © 2000 News World Communications, Inc. Reprinted with permission of The Washington Times.

$200 billion dollars a year, <u>with all but a very small part of it coming out of the Social Security retirement fund.</u>

In fact, the odds (which we will look at soon, when we look at Congress's history of spending) are that the only surplus that there will ever be in "the" (unified) budget will in fact be there *only* from Social Security.

Through 1999, Congress had managed to spend every penny that it could borrow from this Social Security surplus, and had never paid a bit of it back. It enabled them to spend far beyond their own income, to raid the retirement fund, and to keep the public convinced that "The Budget" was in balance!

Don't go any further until you understand all of that absolutely and completely. It has been a monstrous scam, and you need to know about it so it can be stopped.

The laws, as they have always been and still are, say that any surplus of cash in the Social Security "trust fund" *must* be loaned to only one organization: in effect, Congress. We will certainly come back to this subject.

A comparison to private business accounting

As Gene Epstein said in an outstanding March 1, 1999 cover story in Barron's entitled, "HEY GUYS, THERE IS NO BUDGET SURPLUS":

> "If a publicly traded company were to try a scheme like the one now being used in Washington, its top officers would be laughed off Wall Street — or taken away in handcuffs."

Outside of government, in the accounting that private businesses and trust funds use, the law is very specific as to how their books must be totally separated from each other and managed by different people.

The corporation itself, the business, has its own responsibility to provide a product or service and to make a profit. Its board, its officers and its managers have that responsibility to the shareholders. The corporation has to produce revenue, pay bills, and have something left over as profit to reward the risk-taking investors.

Part of the corporation's expense may be to send money over to the retirement trust fund, but when that money is sent, it goes out of the possession or control of the business and goes into the possession and responsibility of the trustees.

These trustees have an entirely separate legal responsibility, not to the business, but to those present or future retirees who have *entrusted* the investment of their retirement funds in these trustees, so that this money will grow in value and be there when the retirees need it.

The bank accounts of the trustees have to be entirely separate from the bank accounts of the business. The trustees are to be totally independent. They have a "fiduciary" responsibility (that is, based on faith or trust) to their retirees.

In the realistic, financial, business world, trustees have to give fiduciary attention to the credit worthiness of those to whom they loan. They have to ask, "What are the odds of our not only collecting interest income on the money that we loan out, but of our then getting paid back?" They are not to take chances on these subjects.

It's actually quite different in the Social Security and other government accounting.

The "trustees" of the Social Security funds are called that, and legally they are in fact trustees. But they are certainly not independent. Three of the six trustees are in fact also in the President's cabinet: the secretaries of labor, treasury, and health and human services, and two others are appointed by the President.

These trustees, by law, have no choice as to what they do with their excess cash. They are required to loan it to only one debtor, regardless of how creditworthy that organization (Congress) is. The loans sound very safe and sound as described by the trustees. The loans buy special "bonds," which however aren't marketable, meaning that they are special IOUs. The interest that they are supposed to earn is not paid in cash to the Social Security trust funds but is simply entered in the Social

Security books as an additional IOU.

What all of this unfortunately leads to is many public statements that conveniently ignore the simple but enormously important point that this debtor (the "on-budget" government, owing money to Social Security) has a record of never being able to pay back what it has borrowed *or* the interest due on it.

So the people who are counting on the "trustees" of the Social Security "trust" funds are told that there is no problem. For example, no problem "until the year 2037." The big assumption in those statements is that the trust fund will in fact be paid back. When we get to the subject of Social Security, we will deal with those prospects in more detail.

We've already looked at the record of our Congress being unable to stay within its own budget. There is nothing in those "On-Budget" budgets yet that shows any actual surplus large enough to be paying back what Congress has already borrowed from the Social Security trust fund.

Congress's record on spending

So let's look at the spending history of Congress. Did it happen during the terms of only certain presidents, or during only those times when one party or the other controlled Congress? It seems that all we hear from Washington is about how they are cutting spending and staying within strict "budget caps." So look at Chart 6-1, page 69. This Chart shows the actual history of our on-budget government's Receipts (income) and Outlays (expense) over the last 30 years and for the estimated next 5 years.

You can almost lay a ruler on the "Outgo" line and draw a straight line through it, covering the entire 35 years. Spending going nowhere but right straight up. No variation to speak of, regardless of which party controlled Congress or who was the

What Are the Facts about the Federal Budget? 69

CHART 6-1: The Outlays and Receipts of the "On-Budget" United States Government, (i.e., Excluding the "Off-Budget" Social Security Outlays and Receipts), Years 1970 through 1999 actual, and 2000 through 2005 estimated

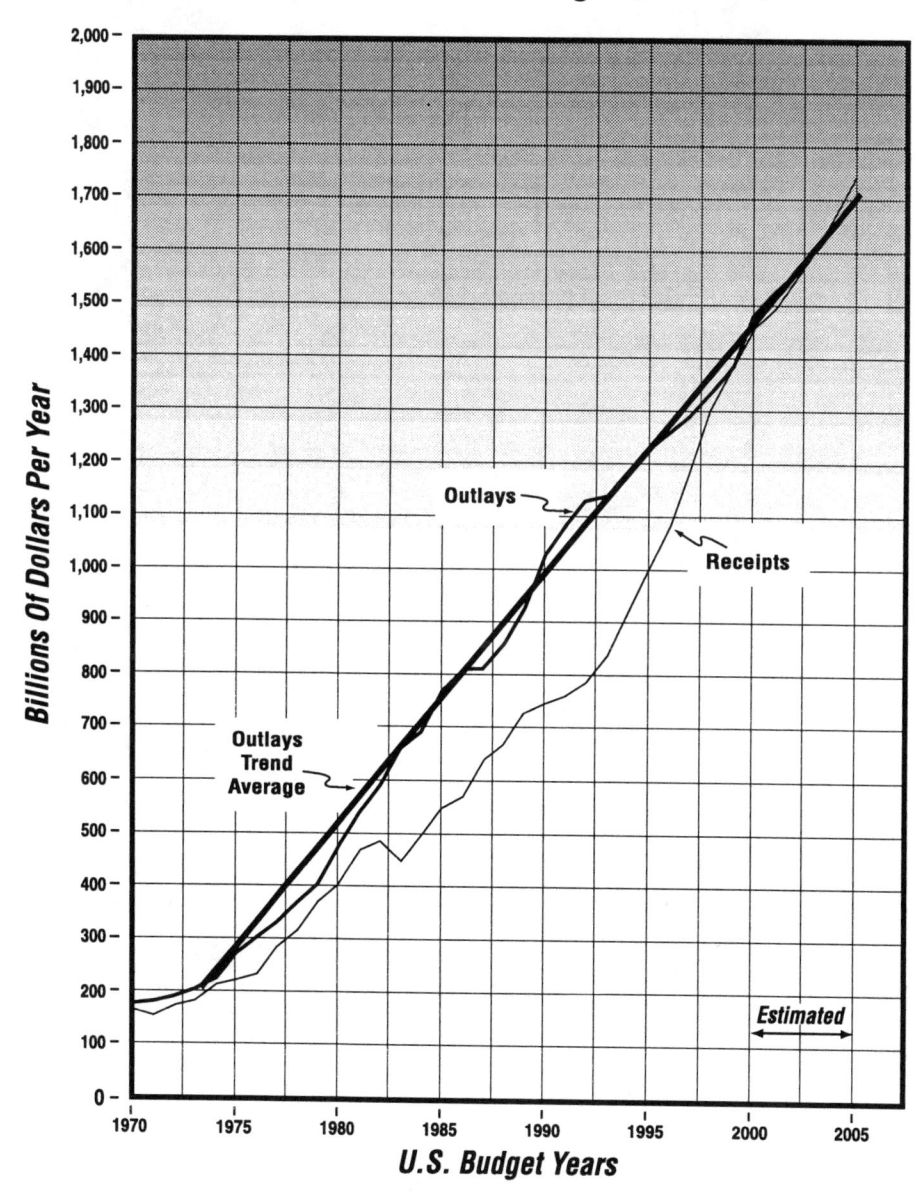

Source: Page 20, The Budget of the United States Government for Fiscal Year 2001, Historical Tables, U.S. Government Printing Office

70   SAVING SOCIAL SECURITY (FROM CONGRESS)

President. No estimates of cutting any rate of increase in spending in the future, either. Ever onward and upward.

One aspect of the perpetual increase in government spending has been a state of mind in Washington that certain government spending was "mandatory," mainly because it was on "entitlements." To believe that some of us are "entitled" to have money spent on us (such as for our health and welfare) had become such an accepted part of political thinking that these costs were classified as essentially "untouchable," if anyone was looking for a way to cut spending. These costs were "mandatory" and just not to be considered. Fortunately, as time goes on, that terminology is having to give way to financial reality — that reality being that nobody is "entitled" to anything if there is no money left to pay for it any more.

Another example of "spin" in financial terminology has been the substitution of the word "investment" for "spending." If a politician says that money is being spent, that is the harsh reality. So it is smoother to say that the money is being "invested," the implication being that the money will not only go out, but there will be returns on that money. In financial terminology, returns on investment are usually measured by specific dollars coming directly back to the person or agency that made the financial investment. Hopefully, when people "spend" money, they get something for what they spent. But that does not make it an "investment." Spending is spending. A spade is a spade.

The limits Congress puts on its own spending

Congress has tried every kind of way to limit its own spending, recent examples having been the Gramm-Rudman-Hollings legislation and various "spending caps." But nothing works for more than a year or so. Routine events (such as the entirely predictable need to pay to take the census) suddenly are rede-

SAVING SOCIAL SECURITY (FROM CONGRESS)

"You seem to have an uncontrollable desire to spend money ... you're lucky you work for the government."

fined as "emergencies," so they can provide an excuse for spending more than Congress promised itself just months earlier.

Right now, Congress is carried away with the idea that there are big surpluses just over the horizon, and fiscal discipline is the last thing on anyone's mind. The question seems to be only what to do with all that will be left over. If you have understood only a part of what you have already read, you know that that is the wrong question.

Finally, we are frankly getting conned by our representatives and senators in Washington into trusting that the money in Social Security is now safe (from Congress itself, that is) for the first time –because it is in a *"lock box"!* To reveal that sham for the nonsense that it is, we need only understand that it takes only a majority of Congress (or maybe a bit more than a majority in the Senate) voting that they need to get back into that "lock box" – and of course, for what are acclaimed to be very valid needs and national purposes — and the box is not only wide open but history. The truth is that Congress can get its hands back into that cookie jar the minute it wants to.

The most ridiculous aspect of all of this is that in the 106th Congress, our senators and representatives spent their time on at least *forty* "lockbox" and "safe deposit box" bills, *not one of which would have been necessary if the money had never gotten out of the Social Security fund and into Congress's hands in the first place!*

They have been trying to decide how to agree to make it a law, that they themselves are to follow, that requires them to keep their own hands off all that Social Security money. No wonder they can't agree on anything that would actually work!

As can be confirmed by your looking back at the excerpt of the "On-Budget, Outlays" in Table 6-1 on page 60, Congress's spending has *more than doubled* in the 15 years from 1984 to 1999 (from $686 billion to $1 trillion 382 billion per year).

Enough about spending. Let's look at the income.

The on-budget income

Then if you look again at the last Chart 6-1 on page 69, covering 35 years of our government's income and expense, you will notice that, starting in 1994 and going through 2000, the income line suddenly took off and went essentially straight up.

In fact, the Receipts (the income) in 1994 totaled $923 billion and in the year 2000 were expected (per this budget) to be $1 trillion 479 billion. That is a *60%* increase in tax income in just six years!

If we are coming close to achieving a surplus in the operations of our government (without using Social Security to do it),

Saving Social Security (from Congress)

it has been accomplished by raising taxes, not by cutting any spending.

Another point that you need to note is that the income of the federal government is basically from *income* tax. If the government itself needs more revenue, it gets it from income tax. Social Security, on the other hand, gets its income from *payroll* taxes. Two different organizations, two separate sources of income. As we will cover later, you need to watch out for efforts to mix these two up.

The impact of capital gains taxes on income

But let's also take a closer look at where at least one part of that income is coming from. The majority of the government's ("On-Budget") receipts in the year 1999 were from individual income taxes. But it is worth taking a moment to see how much of that income was from *capital gains.*

Back in 1991, the capital gains revenue was around $25 billion. Since then, though, we have had the most exceptional decade in the history of the U.S. stock market. The result has been that capital gains tax revenue going to the government has kept going on up, until it was around $100 billion in 1999.

That increase in capital gains tax revenue has certainly been a big help to the government in bringing its total revenues up in the last decade until they are close to expenses. But it is certainly not conservative to think that the market is going to keep going up like that forever, taking capital gains taxation right on up with it. A little bit of budget conservatism might allow for the expectation that capital gains revenue could possibly go back down – thereby putting a considerable crimp in any plans that Congress has for ever having a real surplus in its own accounts.

Copyright © 2000 News World Communications, Inc. Reprinted with permission of The Washington Times.

How the deficits increase debt, and we therefore have increasing interest expense on the borrowing that Congress has to do

If you again go back and look at Table 6-1 on page 60, find the column in the middle of the page for "On-Budget, Surplus or Deficit(-)," where the figure at the top of the column is −72,715. (That means that the government, not counting Social Security, spent 72 billion 715 million more than its revenue that year, and therefore had a "deficit" that big for the year).

When the government doesn't have enough money to pay its bills (which is the situation when it has a deficit), it has to find the money *some*where. Let's see how much money they would have had to go out and find in the 20 years, 1980 through 1999. In other words, if we totaled all the figures in that column, starting with −72,715 down through 724, what was the total deficit for the 20 years?

The answer (in approximate billions!) is $3 trillion 721 billion. You can see this accumulating deficit in Chart 6-2, page 78. They were short that much and had to find it somewhere. So they borrowed it from two places: (1) the Social Security trust fund and (2) the public.

As a matter of fact, they "borrowed" $817 billion of it from the Social Security trust fund and they then borrowed the other $2 trillion 904 billion from the public. That tends to create a very large interest expense.

To say it one more time, our government's borrowing went up by almost $4 trillion dollars in the 20 years through 1999.

There are two results. One is that the government now owes the Social Security trust funds about a trillion dollars. The other is that the government *also* owed the public another $3 trillion 632 billion at the end of fiscal 1999.

The more that Congress borrows, the more annual interest expense it has to pay on that borrowing, and of course then the greater problem it has in keeping its expenses less than its income.

First, Congress borrows from Social Security and has interest expense on that borrowing. They tell Social Security to "put it on the tab," and therefore add to the borrowing and increase the interest expense. Then Congress still needs more money, so it borrows from the public and has real interest expense that

CHART 6-2: Cumulative U.S. Government "On-Budget" Deficits (i.e., Excluding Social Security surpluses or deficits, which are "off-budget"), for 20 Years, 1980 through 1999

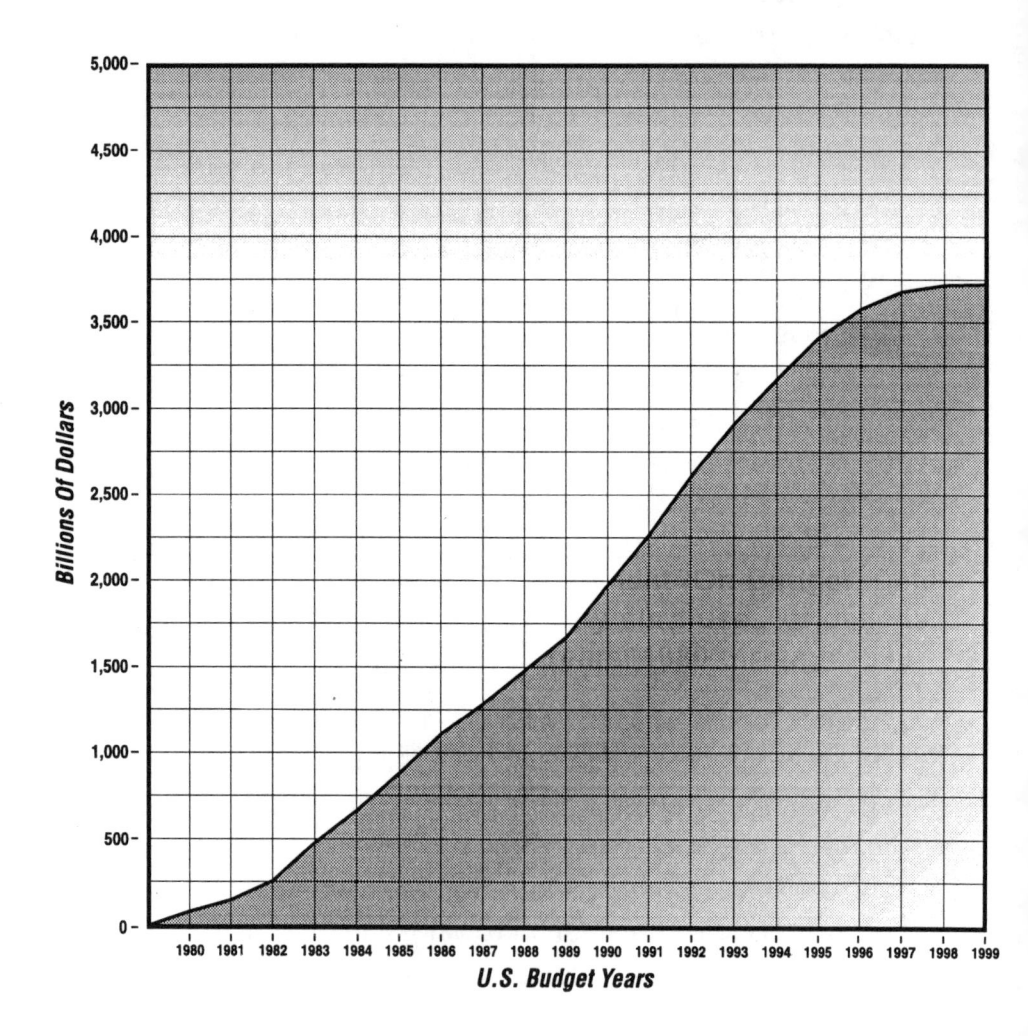

Source: Page 20, The Budget of the United States Government for Fiscal Year 2001, Historical Tables, U.S. Government Printing Office

it really has to pay on that borrowing (even if it has to borrow more in order to have enough to pay the interest).

Chart 6-3, Page 80, shows the trend of the annual gross "interest on the public debt," which is the interest expense Congress has in total from borrowing from *both the* Social Security funds (and any other trust funds) and from the public.

That interest expense, caused by Congress not staying within its own budgets but instead spending so much that it has to keep borrowing more from both the Social Security trust funds and the public, has gone up from being less than $75 billion in 1980 to being $354 billion in 1999 –and with further increases in the budget for at least the next five years.

This "interest on the public debt" was *over 25% of the expense (and the income, for that matter) of our government* (this time, leaving Social Security out of those expense and income totals) in the year 1999. (Specifically, it was $354 billion out of $1 trillion 382 billion).

In fact, interest on the public debt has been more than 25% of each year's outlays (expenses) of our federal government in every year in the last decade.

The source for any paydown of that debt, that borrowing – with the debt of course being the cause of the interest expense in the first place—has to be a real surplus on the "on-budget" books of the government itself. That means more income tax revenue or reduced spending. Otherwise, there is no real surplus from which to pay back Social Security or to ever pay down the additional borrowing from the public.

All of this borrowing sets up *another* game that Congress plays, is playing right now, and which you need to know all about. The way you will hear about it first, from Congress, is that they are *"paying down the public debt."* There is tricky stuff going on here, but you can understand it without too much effort.

If you are in Congress, here is how you do it. You can't keep

CHART 6-3: Annual Gross Interest Expense (not cumulative, but annual), On-Budget United States Government, for the 20 years, 1980 through 1999, actual, as of the end of fiscal years; Interest on the Public Debt

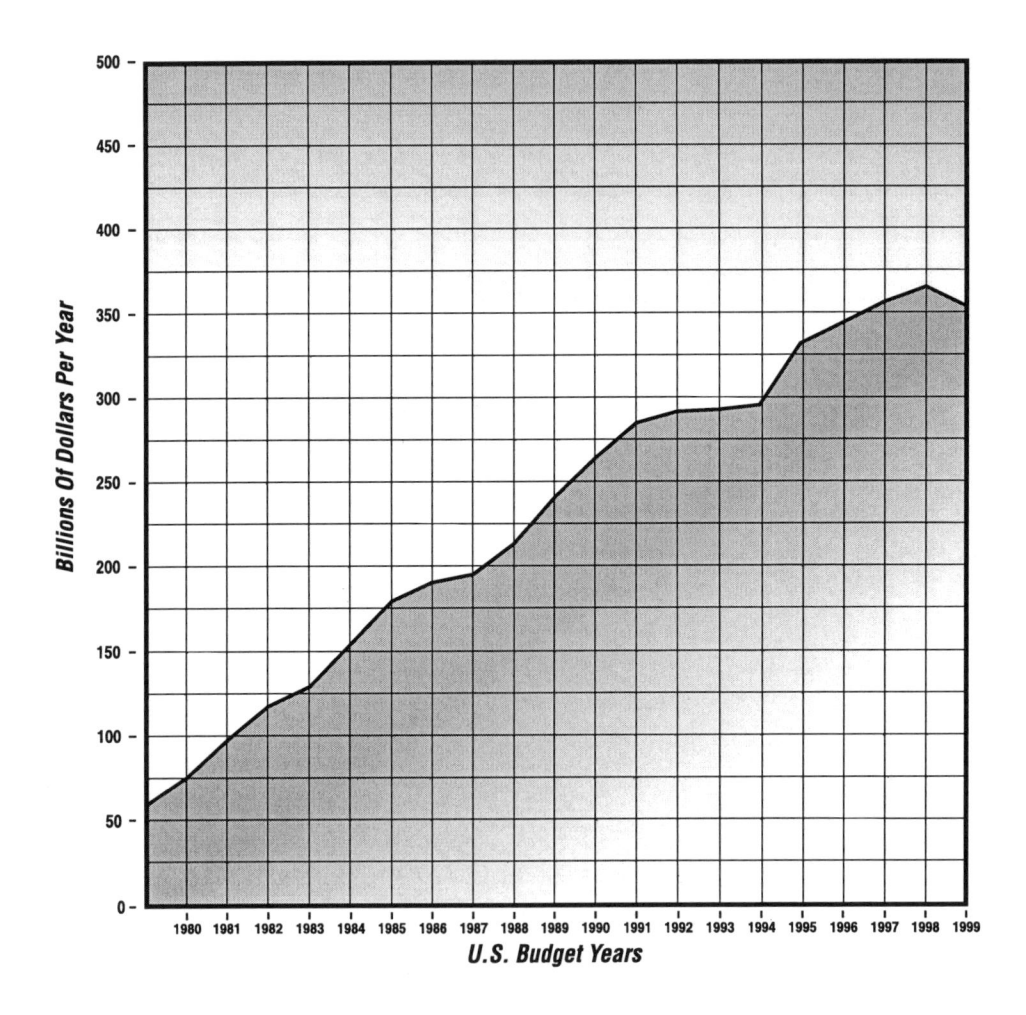

Source: Pages 123-125, The Budget of the United States Government for Fiscal Year 2001, Historical Tables, U.S. Government Printing Office

from spending, so you run a deficit of, let's say, $50 billion in your own ("on-budget") books. But you borrow $150 billion from Social Security. So you have an extra $100 billion. So you pay off some of your debt to the *public.* Sound the trumpets! Congress is paying down the debt!

Of course they actually, in effect, did *two* things: (1) they borrowed $150 billion from Social Security and used it to pay off the public debt, and then (2) they borrowed $50 billion of it back to cover their own overspending.

This is what can go on when the on-budget books of the government are put together with the (supposed-to-be) "off-budget" books of the Social Security trust funds.

As long as this accounting is kept together, the hanky panky will go on.

How is Congress going to pay back what it owes Social Security?

So how is Congress going to (1) pay the Social Security trust fund in cash (not in IOUs) for the interest it owes on what it is borrowing from the trust fund, (2) pay back the approximate $1 trillion, the money itself, that Congress has already borrowed from the trust fund, and (3) be able to get along without borrowing more from the Social Security trust fund (which amounts would also have to be paid back, with interest)?

There are really only two possible answers: either (1) Congress would have to borrow more from the public (with the resulting further increase in annual interest expense) or (2) it would have to actually create a real surplus in its own books. And the only way to do that would be for Congress to have expenses that are less than its tax income.

So we are talking about the need for Congress to not only *balance* its *own* books (that is, have income of its own that is at

Saving Social Security (from Congress)

82

least as great as its own expenses) but to run big *surpluses* (obviously, by having expenses be considerably *less* than its tax income) –surpluses big enough that they enable Congress to pay everything back to the Social Security trust fund.

Before we move on...

Those are only the basic facts of the federal budget. But if you do understand what you have just read, you are better informed than probably 90% of the American public.

The real problem, though, is that probably about 60 million of us need to have this basic understanding of the facts of our federal budget before we are well-enough informed to move on to other facts that we need to all know (such as about Social Security itself and about investing) before we can then start being ready to do some real decision-making about the future of Social Security.

So as we all move through the steps of the necessary decision-making process, we need to stop at this point and make sure that we are all together, that we do understand the facts thus far, that we are not leaving too many people behind, but that enough of us do in fact fully grasp these basics, so we are ready for the next step.

...let's check that we all understand.

We shouldn't be leaving this subject of the federal budget (at least as it pertains to Social Security) until we are sure we understand...

...the difference between "off-budget" (Social Security) and "on-budget (everything else in our federal government), and the way that lumping these two together confuses us.

...the difference between a Social Security surplus and a surplus in the budget of the rest of the government.

...that we want the press, the media and our politicians always to make it very clear which "surplus" they are talking about.

...where the supposed past "surpluses" really came from.

...that our government owes the Social Security retirement trust fund nearly a trillion dollars, either because it borrowed that money or also because it owes the Social Security trust fund for the interest on that borrowed money.

...that the Social Security trust fund is required by law to loan its excess cash to only one organization: the U.S. government, where those funds are then at the disposal of Congress.

...that when we hear that Social Security has invested its excess cash in special "bonds" ("investments in interest-bearing securities of the U.S. government or in securities guaranteed by the United States"), that means that Social Security's accumulated cash is being stored in a cookie jar in Congress—and that the cookie jar is empty.

...how (leaving Social Security out of this), our government's spending has never gone down, has gone up at a constant rate, and shows no real signs of slowing down. In fact, the competition to spend seems to be escalating in Congress.

...that none of us is "entitled" to anything from the others of us, nor is it "mandatory" that we make any such payments if we don't have the money.

...that spending "caps" have not "capped" anything, that no efforts by Congress to restrain its spending –especially by really taking Social Security "off-budget"—have succeeded for more than a few months.

...that the recently ballyhooed "lockbox" is another sham of the same sort.

...how our government's income, from our personal and corporate income taxes, has gone up spectacularly in the last few years.

...that it is the increase in tax revenue, and not any decrease in spending, that has brought income and expense closer together.

...that the government is supposed to get its income from income tax (and not payroll taxes), and Social Security is supposed to get its income from payroll taxes (not income taxes).

...that the surge in capital gains taxes is a significant part of the increase in the government's income, and that continuing such increases aren't something that should be counted on.

...that our on-budget government forecasts almost no surplus at all of its own, and that this forecast is undoubtedly greatly overoptimistic.

...how continuing on-budget deficits have increased the

government's borrowing from both the Social Security fund and the public, meaning that the government's interest expense has kept going up until it is now over 1/4 of each year's on-budget expense.

...that the only real way to get that on-budget interest expense down is to get the debt (money borrowed by Congress from the public) down, and that the only way to get the debt down is to have the money to do that.

...that getting that money will mean that the government itself (without using Social Security's money) will need to have expenses far below its own income.

...that, similarly, the only way that the on-budget government will be able to pay back what it has borrowed from Social Security will be by keeping its own expenses far below its own income.

...that the first question that needs to be asked when reference is made to a "balanced" budget is, "Balanced with what, or with which funds?"

...that when we are told that "the debt is being paid down," we need to ask, "Which debt? The public debt? The money owed to Social Security? And where is the money coming from, to pay this debt down? Is it in fact coming from Social Security?"

...the confusion that has been caused and is still being caused by having the "off-budget" Social Security put together with the "on-budget" government and then presented to the nation as "the" budget.

So, are we ready to continue?

When 60 million of us – give or take a few million — *really, truly* understand what you have just read, it will be an actual revolution in our comprehension of what our federal government has been doing with our money. It is all essentially so simple. But hardly *any* of us have understood it.

And we are not going to be ready to move on to the task of dealing with Social Security until we *do* understand our federal government's finances, because they are so very much a part of the problems of Social Security.

So have all of us recovered from the shock of understanding the real facts of our federal budget, at least as they pertain to Social Security? Only if we *have* gotten all of this clear, are we ready to move on to an equally disturbing set of facts about Social Security itself.

Question #7

What Are the Facts about Social Security?

In looking at the way that money goes from Social Security to the government, you've already looked at the concept of "trustee." The Social Security trustees aren't really independent. They are actually mainly employed, not by the trust, but by "the company." They really have no option as to how or where to invest their funds, because the laws make them loan their money to one organization (in effect, Congress), regardless of whether Congress has ever paid its bill, paid back any of its loans, or every shown itself "credit worthy."

So a Social Security "trustee" is not like a trustee of private funds, is not a trustee as the term is usually understood in the financial community (other than as a legal fiction), and could rightly claim to have no responsibility at all for what has happened or is going to happen. Why? "Because it is really *Congress* that calls all the shots, not the trustees."

The second concept that you need to review is that "trust fund." It does exist, as a legal fiction. But it is closer to the actual truth to say, "There *is* no trust fund."

That's because there is no money in it. As you understand by now, all that is in the "trust fund" (which is neither a fund, or something you can trust to be there) is a bunch of IOUs from Congress (for what they have borrowed from Social Security and for the interest that they haven't paid on that borrowing).

The value of this "fund" is totally dependent on whether Congress can pay Social Security back. And Congress has never been able to do that before.

Also in review, you know now that those IOUs are officially called "special Treasury bonds." Nobody else would buy one, because no one is allowed to. These are strictly IOUs by Congress to Social Security.

And you also know that the "interest income" of Social Security is just another type of IOU. Social Security charges Congress for the money being loaned to Congress, but Congress simply puts that bill "on the tab" with what it already owes.

Social Security charges Congress for the money it is loaning to Congress, using a "market" interest rate, which is now around 6 or 7%. If that interest is ever to be paid to the Social Security fund, it will of course have to be paid by Congress, which means that it comes from income taxes.

One of the ideas that some economists have come up with to increase the amount in the trust fund is for Social Security to simply charge Congress a higher rate for this borrowing. For example, why not make it 10% (or whatever)? That will make it look like Social Security has more money.

This is really brilliant economics. The net effect is that it artificially jacks up the interest rate for Congress, which will have to cover this added interest expense with increased *income* taxes – or, of course, with further borrowing from Social Security! This "simple" answer is, in effect, to raise income taxes, in order to make Social Security look better.

The basic problem with all of this is of course that Congress isn't paying any of this interest expense to Social Security anyway. It all just goes on the tab. But every year that it *stays* on that tab is another year in which interest expense makes up more than 1/4 of Congress's spending.

So let's expand your Social Security vocabulary, starting with "FICA." Those are the letters that stand for the act that created Social Security. You've maybe heard payroll taxes called "FICA taxes," because that's what they are.

When Social Security was first introduced, it was really disguised as something that it wasn't. And, believe it or not, that disguise has kept on working since. Those letters "FICA" stand for "Federal Insurance Contribution Act." It *is* a federal act, but what you put into it isn't a contribution, and what you get for that "contribution" isn't insurance.

A total of 7.65% of your taxable income comes out of your paycheck for Social Security and Medicare. That is your FICA "contribution." It is in fact payroll tax. It is a *tax*.

But you have been taught so well to think of it as not a tax, but a "contribution," that you include that amount in your taxable income when you calculate and pay *income tax* on it too.

You pay a tax on a tax you have already paid.

But surely your "contribution" bought you some definite "insurance"? Well, yes and no. Not "insurance" as you normally think of it, as in insurance of your car, your house or your life.

In those cases (your car, house or life), you have a very definite contract that spells out exactly what you get, under what circumstances, and at what cost. But with Social Security, any relationship between what you pay and what you get is – and you will find this hard to believe at first — simply luck.

Over the 60 years or more in which Social Security has been paying benefits, the benefits have changed so many times that it would take a separate book to spell them all out. One major change, for example, was in 1972, when the benefit schedule was changed so it thereafter increased with prices and wages. But the change turned out to have been made in error. So it was changed again, later.

As to the income side of Social Security, the story is even more complicated, mainly because you are never paying for your own benefits, although most of us have been led to believe we are. You are always paying for someone else's benefits. Periodically, Congress realizes that there isn't enough money coming in to cover benefits for those older people, so they change the payroll taxes to try to catch up.

They may change the taxes by raising the rate on everybody or by raising the rate so a higher and higher amount of each person's income is taxed. And over the years the *benefits* have been tipped to be a higher percentage of the income of lower income people and a lower percentage of the income of higher income people. In other words, if you make less money (and therefore have contributed less money to Social Security), you will get more Social Security benefits (such as, for example, 56% or more of your working income), compared to a high income person, who might get 34% or less of working income.

It is more accurate to say that it is a retirement income welfare program. Those who work pay the bills, and those who are retired get the benefits, and any relationship between what any individual pays in over a lifetime and what that person gets during retirement is just an accident.

When calculations are done to show a "return on investment" based on (1) what a person put into Social Security (through payroll taxes) over a lifetime of working and (2) what that person then receives during retirement, this is a phony calculation that perpetuates a fallacy. Yes, it can be an interesting comparison, but the two (what you paid for, and what you get) really had nothing to do with each other.

We'll come back to this point later, but for now we'll move on to the idea that you may have "an account" in Social Security in which your money is being held or is earning, just for you. You do, after all, have a Social Security *number*, and that must be your *account* number. Think again.

Social Security does in fact keep track of your taxable income over the years, and if you live to retire, some of those years will be part of a very complex formula used to figure out what retirement income to pay you (depending on what the benefits are when you retire). But what you are counting on is the formula that applies when you retire. You do *not* have an account with your name on it in the Social Security system somewhere, with any money in it in your name. You are simply putting money into the big pot to be used to pay the benefits of someone *now*, and later, when you want to retire, you can only hope that (1) the formula pays you enough, and (2) enough people are still working and putting money into the pot to cover what *you* are supposed to get.

If enough people *aren't* still working and putting money in that pot, you are in trouble. And that is what you need to understand very clearly. You are not counting on what *you* put in (which has *nothing* to do with it), but on what *they* are putting in (which has *everything* to do with it).

But you may believe that your benefits are "guaranteed." Well, they aren't. In fact, that issue has been taken to court a *long* time ago and settled quite definitely. In the 1960 case, *Flemming v. Nestor,* the U.S. Supreme Court ruled that workers do *not* have legally enforceable property rights because they have paid payroll taxes. In that case, the Social Security Administration itself even argued to the court that its program was in no sense a federally-administered "insurance program" with guaranteed benefits. If you still believe that, you are simply ignoring the facts. Congress has increased benefits and decreased them, and will clearly need to decrease them again unless significant changes are made in the present program.

This brings us to the phrase "pay-as-you-go," which *does* describe the financing of the Social Security retirement program, and which is one more way of saying that this program is not "insurance." "Pay-as-you-go" is the phrase used most often to try to explain the real way that Social Security collects the money to pay its benefits to retirees.

"Pay-as-you-go" means simply that there is a bill that must be paid for those who are retired and drawing benefits, and that bill is not paid by money that these retirees have set aside (because there *isn't* anything set aside), but is paid by those who are still working (or by those who will be working later, or born later). As time goes by, the workers are to pay whatever that bill is, for those who are no longer working.

That principle worked well in the early days of Social Security when the number of workers was quite high, compared to the number who were retired and drawing benefits. Those who were retired received far, far more than they ever paid into the program.

The problem, of course, is that over the years the benefits

have been greatly increased, the number of retirees is rapidly increasing, that number is increasing also in relationship to the number working, and the very predictable point is coming where those workers will no longer be able to pay-as-they-go.

If that isn't clear, maybe you can think of it as being like a huge unlimited credit card bill, on which your parents, grandparents and their friends are charging monthly, in the expectation that you will be able to "pay-as-you-go" (broke).

The person who has however undoubtedly spelled out this "pay-as-you-go" nature of Social Security the most clearly did it over 20 years ago. Peter J. Ferrara, in his "Social Security, the Inherent Contradiction," absolutely nailed it:

> "The solution of the social insurance paradox is also social security's dirty little secret – the real reason the program exists. The program is a means for the current generation to tax future generations. The initial generation votes for the program because it allows them to tax future generations and thereby pay free benefits to themselves. The first retired generation and a large part of the first working generation are made better off because they get benefits while paying little or nothing themselves in taxes. The future generations, however, are all made worse off because they are burdened with the liabilities of these benefits and locked into a pay-as-you-go system with all of its drawbacks and negative effects. Unlike the first generation, they cannot get free benefits for themselves through the program. Future generations do not vote, and therefore they cannot object to the taxation being imposed on them.
>
> "The real reason for the program is that it allows the initial generation that adopts it to tax future generations to pay free benefits to itself. These free benefits are simply a func-

tion of the pay-as-you-go system. When such a system is begun, huge tax increases are generated with nowhere to go because there are no accrued benefit obligations built on the basis of past tax payments. These tax revenues, however, are not to be saved and invested to pay the future benefits of current taxpayers, as in an invested system. They are therefore paid out to the first generation of retirees as free benefits. The fatal flaw of social security, its operation on a pay-as-you-go basis, is the real reason for its creation in the first place, as well as the real reason why it must ultimately meet its downfall.

"The actual reason for the program's existence is hardly an attractive one. There certainly seems to be something immoral about taxing future generations who do not yet have voices, let along votes, to object. Doing so is nothing more than taxation without representation. Revolutions have been known to occur for similar transgressions. This immorality is especially brazen since the benefits to the first generation are bought at the cost of locking all future generations into a program that makes them more worse off than the first generation is made better off. Seen in this light, the first generation politicians who imposed the program seem less like statesmen and more like demagogues. The program seems less like a method of helping the elderly and more like a giant con game."

You should now be working with a better understanding of the words that are typically used to keep you confused about Social Security. We can then look at the circumstances under which you would actually collect Social Security retirement benefits.

Let's look first at what you yourself would get as benefits.

The main circumstance is of course that (having been a worker) you reach the age of 62 and elect to draw reduced "early retirement" benefits, or that you wait until the age of 65 (or a slowly increasing age, in future years) and start drawing "normal retirement" benefits. (Or you can wait to start drawing benefits until *after* your normal retirement date, and these "delayed retirement" benefits are higher). You receive those benefits monthly, with cost-of-living increases each year, until you die.

If you yourself do not reach retirement age, there are no benefits for you. If you were paying payroll taxes those many years, while working under the illusion that there would be a "payback," you need to remember: no retirement, no retirement benefits for you. (And we are not talking about any change in disability insurance, during your lifetime, which would continue as it is).

However, there would possibly be benefits to your survivors, if you died either before or after you retired: (1) any children would receive benefits through age 18, if unmarried and in school, (2) if you had been married at least 10 years and then divorced, that spouse (if not remarried before age 60) might receive 75% to 100% of what you would have received, based on your working earnings record to date, and it wouldn't affect the benefits of any current spouse that you leave. However, with either spouse, if the benefits from their own working records are higher, then they would get those benefits rather than anything based on your work record. (3) Your spouse (unless the benefits from his or her own work record were higher) would get a survivor's benefit starting no earlier than at age 60 (and reduced if it started that early). There are many, many details, but basically that is it.

In contrast, if a person did not have Social Security and was setting aside money for retirement, but died before (or after) reaching retirement age, that saved and invested amount would be part of the person's property and estate. If there was a need to cover children through age 18, it could be done through (very inexpensive) term insurance. The spouse would be covered by term insurance if necessary, joint-and-survivor coverage on any annuity or by inheriting the savings and being able to continue to earn from investment of them. (The divorced spouse would have to be covered by the divorce agreement or by his or her own earnings and savings).

Something else you have probably been aware of, but which may be worth review, is how most of us have been so influenced by the word "contribution" that we happily pay a tax on a tax. We pay income tax on our payroll tax.

Typically, the 7.65% of your taxable income is taken out as a FICA or payroll tax (for Social Security and Medicare). It is called a "contribution." Your employer also matches the 7.65% with a "contribution" of his own. For the employer, when calculating the corporate income tax, that "contribution" is a deductible expense, so no income tax is paid on it. When you, however, fill out *your* income tax return, that amount that you paid as a payroll tax is recorded as *income*, on which you then pay income tax.

This may be something to keep in mind when we later get to comparisons of staying with Social Security (and continuing to pay payroll taxes, probably at an increasing rate) or leaving Social Security and investing to provide for your own retirement. In the latter case, your contributions to your own savings account would be *deductions* from your taxable income.

It may also be worth noting that there is a separate program, SSI (for Supplemental Security Income), which would *not* be affected by or eliminated by "privatization," and which is not paid for by Social Security but is financed by the government. This is a "safety net" program that already provides, and would continue to provide, income to those whose working histories do not generate even adequate minimum retirement income.

So this gets us to the point of actually looking at how "safe" Social Security is. This paragraph comes from the current (1999) pamphlet, "Social Security Retirement Benefits," put out by the Social Security Administration:

"You also need to know about Social Security's financial stability. Each year, Social Security's Board of Trustees reports on the financial status of the Social Security program. These reports are valuable tools for evaluating and ensuring the economic health of the Social Security system. The latest report indicates that the Social Security system, as currently structured, will be able to pay benefits well into the next century. This means Congress has the time it needs to make changes to safeguard the program's financial future.

"You can count on Social Security being there when you need it."

If one sentence above didn't catch your attention, we might go back and emphasize it:

"This means *Congress has the time it needs to make changes to safeguard the program's financial future.*"

There seems to be a suggestion that there might be some problems.

The year 2037

Those who want to assure us that there is no immediate problem will often refer to the year 2037. They say there is no problem until 2037. We keep hearing "2037" as the magic number. No problems until then.

For example, the authors of "Social Security, the Phony Crisis" start their book right off by saying:

> "The program will take in enough revenue to keep all of its promises for over 30 years, without any changes at all.
>
> "The Social Security trust fund loans its annual surplus, now running at over $124 billion, to the federal government. The surplus, which has been accumulating since 1983, when the payroll tax was increased, will help finance the baby boomers' retirement, which is why the program will not have any trouble meeting its obligations while the boomers are retiring."

You need to understand how phony their assumptions are about that trust fund.

That number "2037" refers, actually, to the combination of two funds: the regular retirement income trust fund (OASI) and the disability insurance trust fund (DI). So the number refers to what is called the OASDI fund (and its income and outgo).

In fact, OASI is by far the larger of the two funds and is due to run out of money in the year 2039, and the DI fund is estimated to run out in the year 2023. But when you hear "2037," they are talking about the two funds totaled together ("OASDI").

So where do people get this "2037" estimate? If you are old enough that you get an annual statement of "Your Estimated Benefits" from the Social Security Administration, you might notice this little sentence on page 2:

> "(2) Your benefit figures shown here are only estimates based on current law, and the laws governing benefit amounts may change because, by 2037, the payroll taxes collected will be enough to pay only about 72 percent of benefits owed."

That little statement might assure some people that there is no problem until 2037, or it might get some of us wondering what happens suddenly in 2037 when the money to pay benefits runs out.

But the annual report of the Board of Trustees of these two funds goes into a little more detail:

"The combined OASI and DI Trust Funds are estimated to be depleted under present law in 2037 based on the intermediate assumptions. At that time, the estimates indicate that annual tax revenues would be sufficient to cover 72 percent of annual expenditures.

"....the funds are exhausted in 2037, 3 years later than estimated in last year's report."

"Intermediate assumptions"? As a matter of fact, the trustees make three projections, or estimates, of what will happen in the future. Those three are called "optimistic," "intermediate," and "pessimistic." (Later, we can look at how accurate these estimates have been in the past. But for now, let's just look at this particular "2037" estimate).

So the 2037 estimate is just one of three estimates. It is the middle estimate of the three. Among other things, we might also want to look at the "pessimistic" assumption, so we also know how bad they think things might get.

What the actuaries of these funds estimate for you are basically (1) the expected income into the fund, (2) the expected outgo or payouts of the fund, (3) what the difference is between these two numbers, and (4) what happens with any money that comes in, in excess of payouts.

The annual outgo of these funds is basically straightforward. It is the payment of benefits, either to those retired or those disabled.

But the "income" in any given year comes mainly from 4 sources: (1) The first and biggest source of income is payroll taxes: usually 5.3% of your gross income (for retirement) and 0.9% (for disability), and a matching 5.3% and 0.9% from your employer. A total amount equal to 12.4% of your taxable income. (2) The second source of income is that the IRS now charges income taxes on Social Security benefits and sends that money back to the Social Security fund. It is a roundabout way of reducing benefits on those who make more money and therefore pay income taxes, but this taxation of benefits does come back into the trust funds. (3) The third source of "income" happens when the Social Security funds have more money in the bank than they need to pay out immediately. They "loan" it to the U.S. government, charge the government interest (currently at a rate of about 6-7%) for use of that money, and make an entry in the Social Security fund books that says, in effect, "This is income, because they owe it to us, although it hasn't been paid yet – (and never has been)." (4) And fourth, when the Social Security funds are more than Social Security needs to pay out immediately, they loan those funds to the U.S. government and then expect to get the loans themselves paid back (although it has never happened) to use to cover the deficit – the gap — between income and expense in future years when there isn't enough income to cover expenses.

Let's think of this "income" in two categories: real cash and not real cash. The cash, or real income is the money that actually comes into these funds from the above-covered (1) payroll taxes and (2) income tax on the benefits. That is actually money being transferred, so it is in the bank to be used to cover "outgo." But the rest, the "not cash" part is one enormous IOU from the rest of the government. It will not in fact be "income" to these Social Security funds unless the U.S. government pays back both the borrowed amounts and the interest due on them to Social Security.

What Are the Facts about Social Security?

We have to realize that this is a monstrous "IF," given that the entire history of the relationship between the Social Security trust funds and the U.S. government has been that the latter has spent every penny it could get out of the trust funds, has never paid any of it back, is only *beginning* to forecast "surpluses" on its own books, but is actually scrambling to find more and more ways to keep spending more, in order to use up its own "surpluses" before they even occur.

Because the Social Security trustees themselves realize this major difference between (1) cash income and (2) total "income" (this total including the amounts yet to be received from the U.S. government, those amounts being in large part or possibly all wishful thinking), they oblige us by showing their estimates of the future not only on a total income basis, but also on just a real cash basis.

So Chart #7-1 on page 104 shows what the trustees expect as (1) income, total from only actual *cash* sources: payroll taxes and income tax on benefits, and (2) actual expected outgos.

This chart shows trillions of dollars per year on the scale up the left side, and the years 2000 through 2040 across the bottom.

For now, skip the dash lines and look at only the two solid lines, which are the "intermediate" estimates that the funds will stop having enough money in "2037."

As you can see, on the "intermediate" estimates, the cash outgo line crosses over the cash income line in the year 2015. And after that, the outgo line stays above the income line, and it keeps getting further and further above the income line.

In fact, by the year 2036, the cash outgo per year is expected to be one trillion dollars (or 36%) more than the cash income! And, you can see that the gap between the cash income and the cash outgo is still getting greater. But the trustees usually stop showing the numbers after the year 2037, because after that the situation is truly impossible.

104   SAVING SOCIAL SECURITY (FROM CONGRESS)

CHART 7-1: Estimated OASDI (Old-Age, Survivors and Disability Income) Outgo and Income (excluding interest income), Calendar Years 2010-2045

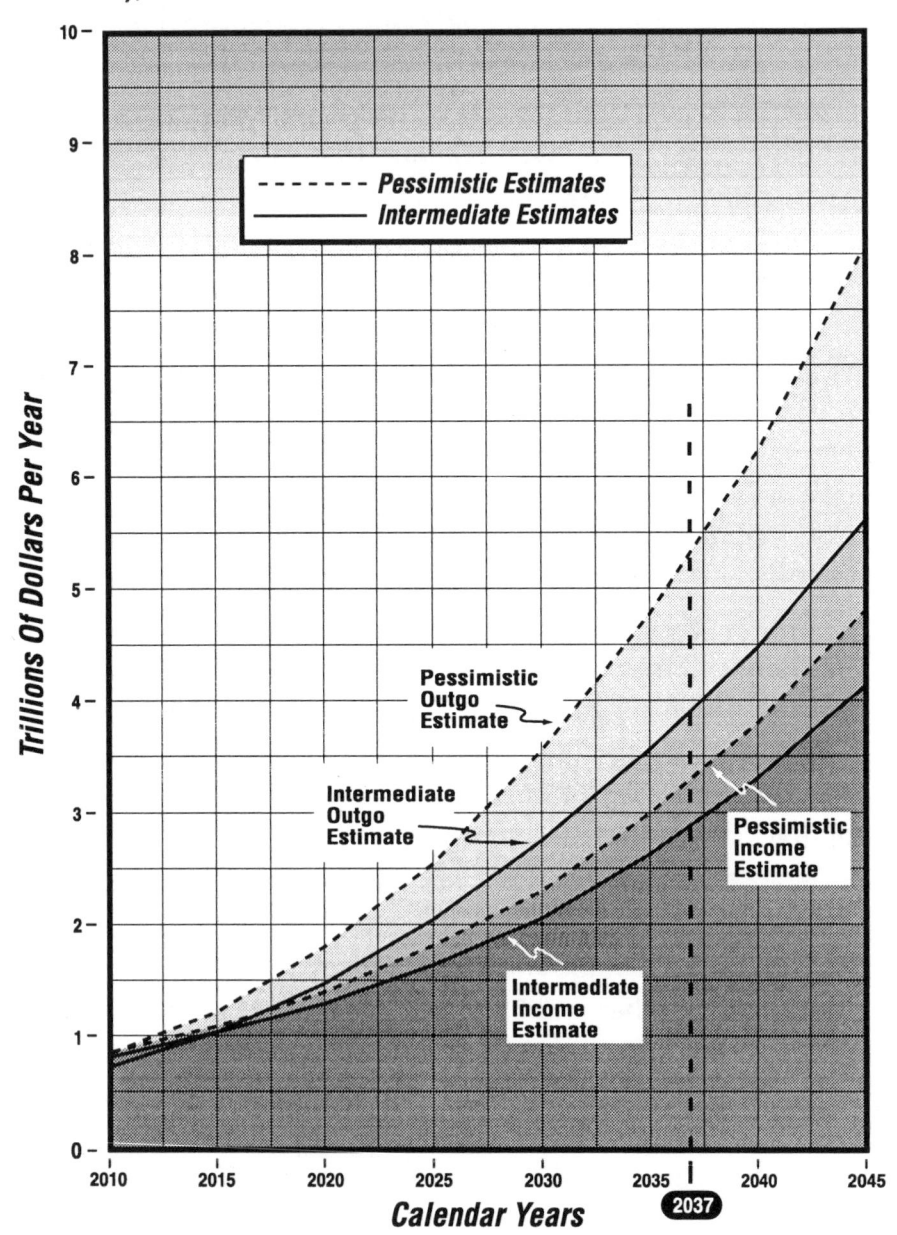

Source: Pages 183-4, The 2000 Annual Report of the Board of Trustees of the Federal Old-Age and Survivors Insurance and Disability Insurance Trust Funds, U.S. Government Printing Office

To say it another way, the known sources of <u>cash</u> income (payroll taxes and income tax on benefits) <u>stop covering the outgo in the year 2015</u>, and after that there won't be enough money to pay full benefits to those on Social Security unless these two Social Security funds can get repaid the money borrowed (principal AND interest) by the U.S. government.

If you didn't understand that paragraph, loud and clear, re-read it and make sure you do, because it is very important.

Those repayments from the U.S. government will have to come from either of two sources: either the government will have to raise income taxes, or it will buy time by borrowing the money, running up a bill in the form of even more interest expense (which is already a major portion of our annual government expenses), and then trying to pay back these borrowed amounts later, by raising taxes <u>then.</u>

In other words, the two possible sources are income taxes then or income taxes later.

But it is, unfortunately, even a little more complicated than that. We have been talking about getting the government to pay back the trillion or so that it will owe Social Security only up until *now*. What happens between now and the year 2037, between the Social Security trust fund and the government is far, far more important than that.

You remember, from learning the facts about the federal budget, that the Social Security trust funds were running bigger and bigger annual surpluses. Those surpluses, in total, were around $150 billion in the year 2000, headed toward an estimated $213 billion in 2005, and getting bigger every year.

We're going to shift gears here, in order to talk about the future of just the OASI retirement fund. The federal budget shows the surpluses in *all* the Social Security trust funds, and we have been talking about the "2037" that refers to the OASDI (retirement plus disability) fund.

But the disability fund is forecast to run out in 2023 and cease to exist. We are also really more interested in what happens to that retirement fund, which is much larger and is the one we are really talking about. We know Congress owes the retirement income fund about a trillion dollars already, but then let's look at what is expected to happen in only that OASI retirement fund, starting at the beginning of the year 2001 and going through the end of 203<u>9</u>, when it also supposedly runs out and ceases to exist.

In this OASI retirement fund, the cash surpluses are bigger every year through the year 2008, but there continue to be cash surpluses through 2016. So that builds up the trust fund, and that trust fund, now in the trillions, is being "loaned" to the U.S. government.

But catch this. The interest expense has of course *also* been going up and up, because of a bigger and bigger amount loaned to Congress, and the interest "income" from Congress to this one Social Security fund is expected to be $67 *billion* in the year 2001, going up to $146 *billion* in the year 2008 and $282 *billion* in the year 2016. And it keeps going right on up, to $384 *billion* a year by 2026. Guess where all the money is coming from to be sure we make it to the year 2039?!

Between at the start of the year 2001, and going through 2039 (and actually they don't make it all the way through that year, even on paper), the plan is that the Social Security Administration is going to receive a total of <u>$9 trillion 500 billion</u> of interest income from Congress on the money it has loaned Congress during that time.

And if that doesn't blow your mind, think about this one. The trust fund will keep increasing (in large part, because of putting more and more of this interest on the tab) until it is up to (not the trillion that it is now, but) <u>$6 trillion 166 billion.</u> And for all of those 25 years Congress won't spend a penny of it. And they'll pay it all back. Right.

IF the U.S. government can do all that, then the Social Security disability income fund won't run out of money until the year 2023, the retirement trust fund won't run out of money until the year 2039, but IT WILL STILL BE IN TROUBLE THEN, AND THE TROUBLES WILL KEEP GETTING WORSE.

To say it once more, if the U.S. government pays back EVERYTHING it owes Social Security for interest and principal, then, yes, that will get the disability fund to at least 2023 and the retirement fund to the year 2039, AND, thereafter, the funds will be short of funds to the tune of more than a *trillion* dollars a year! (Not millions or billions. Trillions. Per year. The current *total* budget of the "on-budget" U.S. government, including defense, interest expense, Medicare, etc. – but excluding Social Security, is around $1 trillion 500 billion per year.)

These payments or repayments (by the U.S. government to these two Social Security trust funds) would have to come from a surplus in the books of the U.S. government. In other words, the U.S. government would have to itself cover its already-expected expenses and then raise these additional trillions of dollars of income in order to pay back its debts to the Social Security trust funds.

And this is a U.S. government that has managed to keep increasing its expenditures (its own "outgo") so much that it had a surplus (of its own) in only one year in the 41 years, 1958 through 1998, and which is (with unrealistic optimism) estimating that it will, in the 7 years, 1999 through 2005, run a surplus of only one half of 1% of income, or an average surplus (over those 7 years of ever-increasing revenue) of about $8 billion 600 million per year (before any tax cut).

Another way that the trustees themselves dramatize this shortage-of-income problem for the total OASDI fund in their annual report for the year 2000 is that they say, in effect, "If we don't get paid back by the U.S. government, we will have to keep raising payroll taxes (from their present 12.4% plus income tax on benefits) year after year until the rate is <u>17.87%</u> of taxable payroll in the year 2037 (and headed toward 19.53% of payroll in year 2075)."

So the assurances that we get about no problems until the year 2037 are based on the "intermediate" estimates of the future cash income and outgo of the OASDI Social Security trust funds <u>AND</u> –and that is one enormous "AND"—<u>the probably very unrealistic expectations that (1) hundreds of billions of dollars will be paid back by the U.S. government to the trust funds, that (2) the Congress will not spend any of the additional trillions building up in these trust funds over the next 35 years or more, and that (3) Congress can pay the Social Security trust funds (in cash) nearly $10 trillion in additional interest expense on all of this borrowing.</u>

So let's stop for a moment and summarize. We have been talking about only the "intermediate" assumptions and projections. Those numbers say the OASDI funds run out of <u>cash</u> income in the year 2015 (obviously, only 14 years from now, not 36 years from now). There is no cash in the Social Security trust funds. It has all been loaned to Congress, and Congress spent it all. So to start paying the Social Security trust funds back, starting in the year 2015, Congress is going to have to start generating surpluses of its own for the first time in the last 60 years or so.

If history of the last 60 years is any guidance, this will be totally impossible for Congress to do. The record is that, if they can get their hands on money (and even if they <u>can't)</u> they are going to spend it. We can wish otherwise, but that's not being realistic.

But don't think <u>that</u> is a big problem. "You ain't seen nothin' yet!"

We have been talking about only the "intermediate" projections. Wait until you see what the trustees think the "pessimistic" situation might be!

Let's go back to Chart #7-1 on page 104, but this time look at the two <u>dash</u> lines, because those are the <u>pessimistic</u> estimates made by the trustees' actuaries. The upper dash line is the pessimistic expected outgo, and the lower dash line is the pessimistic expected income.

As you will see later, the actuaries' estimates are the best that they can make, but the later <u>actual</u> results do not always stay within the actuaries' "optimistic" and "pessimistic" high and low estimates.

What the <u>dash</u> lines (the "pessimistic" estimates) say is:

1. These OASDI funds run out of cash in the year <u>2010</u>, only <u>ten</u> years from now,

2. By the year 2035, the outgo will exceed the income by <u>$1 trillion 800 billion per year</u>, with the deficit equaling 60% of income. (In other words, with $1.60 needing to go out for every $1.00 coming in).

3. By the year 2040, that outgo will exceed income by <u>$2 trillion 400 billion per year</u>, with that deficit now up to 64% of income.

And what the trustees' annual report for 2000 shows (although it is off this chart) is that by the year 2075, on this pessimistic set of assumptions, they expect the <u>deficit</u> in these two trust funds to total to <u>$19 trillion 800 billion per year</u>, with that being more than <u>twice</u> the amount of money coming in each year! (And the deficit would – believe it or not — still be growing).

If Social Security had to cover the total outgo with payroll tax income, the payroll tax rate by the year 2075 would have to be

110   SAVING SOCIAL SECURITY (FROM CONGRESS)

ZIGGY

*Ziggy ©Ziggy and Friends Inc.
Reprinted with permission of Universal Press Syndicate. All rights reserved.*

<u>28.29%</u> of taxable payroll! And, if that isn't bad enough, the situation would still be getting worse, year by year.

So now you know how "there are no problems until the year 2037." There are in fact *enormous* cash problems in the OASDI trust funds by the years 2010 or 2015, after which time there will need to be new tax income coming into the Social Security trust funds, either from (1) the U.S. Government (which will presumably not cut expenses, but will therefore need to raise income taxes) or from (2) payroll tax increases.

You may well be asking yourself at this point, "Sure. But how good *are* these estimates that the actuaries make for the trustees? For example, how often do the actual numbers not stay within the optimistic and pessimistic highs and lows?"

Let's look at that.

Comparison of Predictions, 1989 and 2000 Annual Reports

In order to make the best possible predictions about the future status of the Social Security funds, the actuaries compile data on a great number of indicators. For example, they compile historical data and then project it into the future on how many people have been born and will be born each year, and on how many people have died each year and will die each year. This is obviously so they can try to determine how many of us there will be working and paying into Social Security, and how many of us will be retired and drawing benefits from Social Security.

They also then compile historical data on wages, changes in the cost-of-living index, average additional increases in wages and unemployment rates.

Other factors that they study and project are annual interest rates (percent), annual net immigration, marriage and divorce rates and retirement patterns, among other things. Then, with the power of computers, they are able to calculate and project the future from the consolidation of all of this history and these assumptions about the future.

The assumptions that the actuaries make are of course very important, and are given great attention. And in addition, the Social Security Advisory Board called for a 1999 Technical Panel on Assumptions and Methods, that was to give an outsider's review of the Social Security actuaries' work. (That panel concluded that Social Security's assumptions are probably optimistic.) Also, another independent study was done by the accounting firm of PricewaterhouseCoopers, for the General Accounting Office, reviewing the assumptions and methods used by the Social Security actuaries. (That study concluded that, all in all, the trustees' intermediate assumptions were reasonable and based on state-of-the-art techniques).

Beyond that, the annual reports of the trustees spell out all of the detail of the assumptions and the supporting reasoning. So this information becomes the basis of continuing review by economists and the academic community.

But the Social Security trustees are the first to point out that their predictions are not infallible:

> "While it is reasonable to assume that actual future trust fund experience will fall within the range defined by the three alternative sets of assumptions used in this report, no definite assurance can be given that this will occur because of the uncertainty inherent in projections of this type and length.
>
> "....the estimates are only an indication of the expected trend and potential range of future program experience.
>
> "Long-range estimates are subject to much uncertainty and should not be considered precise forecasts. Instead they should be considered as indicative of the general trend and range of costs that could reasonably be expected to occur."

Another way to say it more simply would be:

> "Sure, we make the best educated guesses that we can, and we run those through computers. But let's not kid ourselves. Nobody can really predict the future."

The Social Security actuaries have to forecast 75 years into the future. Think, for example, of how well someone in 1926 could have predicted how things would be in 2001.

To get some idea of how good the predictions (the estimates, the guesses) of the Social Security actuaries are, for example,

What Are the Facts about Social Security?

we can pick the 1989 annual report of the trustees and compare it with their 2000 report, 11 years later.

First, let's look at what they predicted in early 1989 for the year 2000 on 7 major factors, and then what they predicted in early 2000 for the year 2000. (Two of the 7 factors do not show 1999 actual data, so the comparison is to the 2000 estimate, which hopefully isn't too far off when made in early 2000).

Back in 1989, there were two estimates made of the "intermediate" assumptions: These days, there is only one "intermediate" estimate for each year.

Factor Estimated	1989 Estimate of What 2000 Would Be			2000 Estimate
	Optimistic	Intermediate	Pessimistic	of 2000
OASDI, in current dollars, in billions, excluding interest income:				
Income:	$522.4	$532.4-$562.1	$555.9	$500.7
Outgo:	$380.4	$417.6-$457.7	$519.0	$410.3
Social Security Population (thousands):				
20-64:	167,585	166,033	164,585	168,228
65 plus	34,766	35,460	36,113	35,482
Covered Workers (000):	145,795	143,377-142,124	138,702	153,560
OASI Beneficiaries (000):	38,396	38,947-38,944	39,445	38,193
SSA Ave Wage Index:	33,088	34,070	36,343	31,685

So on 5 of these 7 major factors, the expected actual results for the year 2000 are <u>outside</u> the range that the actuaries expected just 11 years ago.

Then we can use the same two annual reports (1989 and 2000) to look at the <u>long-range</u> forecasts. In this case, the 1989 annual report made a forecast of the year 2060, which was then 75 years away. Then, in the 2000 annual report (11 years later), we can see what they forecast <u>now</u> for 2060.

In other words, how much have they changed their minds in 11 years about the year 2060? Let's look at the same 7 factors:

Factors:	Year of Estimate	Optimistic	Intermediate	Pessimistic
OASDI Income:	1989	8,258	9,304-13,886	14,954
	2000	6,997	8,089	9,544
Outgo:	1989	7,641	11,591-18,144	28,233
	2000	7,575	11,384	17,726
Social Security Population				
20-64	1989	215,744	177,163	141,840
	2000	242,561	210,677	183,393
65 plus	1989	67,481	72,868	81,859
	2000	77,354	83,634	92,154
Covered Workers:				
	1989	189,723	152,183-150,606	116,916
	2000	220,671	189,904	163,771
OASI Beneficiaries:				
	1989	70,500	74,475-74,398	81,741
	2000	78,323	83,278	90,374

SSA Ave Wage Index
1989	390,605	536-015-805,613	1,080,066
2000	296,742	392,253	524,066

These differences are no criticism of the actuaries. They simply show the problems of forecasting the future, even with the very best of assumptions.

Another example of these forecasting problems is the date that the actuaries have estimated that the OASDI trust fund would be "exhausted" (meaning, out of money), so benefits couldn't be paid in full. Back in the year 1983, they thought the trust fund would cover outgos until 2063 (that is, <u>80 </u>years in the future). But <u>two years later</u> they figured that the trust fund would be running out in 2048 (that is, in 65 years). By the 1989 report, they had it down to 2046, and by 1995 to 2030. In the 1999 report, they predicted that the money would run out in 2034, but a year later they decided it now looked more like 2037(that being in 37 years).

At a minimum, one observation has to be that they keep finding that the date on which this trust fund runs out of money is generally getting closer. (All of this of course assumes that the money that is supposed to be in the trust fund is <u>in</u> the trust fund, but you now already know about that additional little problem).

The major three actuarial factors: growth of the economy (GDP), fertility, and life expectancy

For good reason, a lot of attention focuses on three factors that the actuaries must forecast. The first of these is the rate at which the economy will grow. The second is how many children will be born (and become workers, paying payroll taxes). The third is life expectancy, or how long we can expect people to live (and be recipients of retirement income benefits).

Growth of the economy (GDP)

Those who want to deny the existence of a Social Security "crisis" say, basically, that if the economy will just keep booming along the way that it has, then that growth will generate enough income to pay for everything, with no problem.

They say the economy has been growing at a rate of 3 or 3-1/2% for the last 75 years, so it is unrealistic to expect that it will drop to (an intermediate forecast rate of) 1.7%, then 1.6%, and by the year 2075, a rate of 1.5%.

The actuaries of the Social Security Administration obviously give great attention to this factor, and their annual reports explain their reasoning in detail. (And, as covered, that reasoning gets reviewed by outsiders, few of whom as a matter of fact have questioned this forecast).

The three factors that account for growth of the economy (as measured by GDP) are (1) labor force growth, (2) productivity growth, and (3) average hours worked.

The main one of these that they expect to make a change is the first one: a slower labor force growth. It is quite predictable from birth rates, which are down significantly. Beyond that, as we'll come to, other analysts think that the birth rates that the actuaries are using are too high.

Essentially, those who question these projections of the slowing rate of growth of the U.S. economy are not accepting the lower birth rates and therefore the resulting slower expected growth rate for the labor force.

Fertility, or birth rates

A second major factor is the rate at which we add children, who then become workers, generating the payroll taxes. The fertility rate is basically the number of children that a woman would have in a lifetime. Back in 1950 and 1960, the U.S. rate was 3.50 and 3.61, but by the year 1976 it was down to 1.74 (about half of what it had been earlier), and for the last decade it has been 2.02 to 2.07.

Starting with the year 2025, the optimistic forecast is that the rate will be 2.20, the intermediate forecast is that it will be 1.95, and the pessimistic forecast is that it will be 1.70

Most of the questioning seems to be whether the rate will drop back toward 1.7, or even lower. That would mean less children, less workers, less payroll taxes.

One answer might come from looking at what the total fertility rate is of other countries in the developed world. The 2000 World Population Sheet of the Population Reference Bureau tells us that the rate is:

More Developed World	1.5
Canada	1.5
Australia	1.7
Singapore	1.5
Hong Kong	1.0
China (other than Hong Kong)	1.8
Japan	1.3
South Korea	1.5
Europe	1.4

Those numbers would certainly confirm that there is every possibility that the U.S. total fertility rate will drop below the 1.95 of the intermediate forecast or even below the 1.70 of the pessimistic forecast. If so, it means less workers, less expected payroll tax income, and a greater problem for Social Security.

Life expectancy, or how long we live

We're going to deal with this subject at a little length, next, but the additional question is whether we will actually live even longer than the actuaries are projecting. There are those who think that our medical advances will keep increasing our life spans, but you will just have to judge for yourself from the following.

Life expectancy is a major factor in what is happening in Social Security, and it has increased more than many of us may realize. For example:

	At Birth		At Age 65	
	Male	**Female**	**Male**	**Female**
In 1940:				
(when SS began)	61.4 yrs.	65.7 yrs.	11.9 yrs.	13.4 yrs.
In 2000:	73.9	79.6	15.9	19.2
Change, 1940-2000	+12.5	+13.9	+4.0	+5.8
In 2075	81.0	85.1	19.9	22.7
Change, 1940-2075	+19.6	+19.4	+8.0	+9.3

So, when Social Security started making payments in 1940, with full normal retirement benefits to start being paid when people reached the age of 65, we have to stop and remember that <u>the average life expectancy (men and women total) wasn't even 65!!</u>

What those above numbers also say is that a man born in 1940 could expect to live, on average, 61.4 years, but that a man born in the year 2000 could expect to live 73.9 years, or 12.5 years longer. A woman born in 1940 could expect to live, on average, 65.7 years, but a woman born in the year 2000 could expect to live 79.6 years, or 13.9 years longer.

For those who have lived to be 65 years old, though, there are expectancies as to how many years more they will live, on average. In 1940, a man who had lived to age 65 could expect to live an average of 11.9 years more. But a man who had lived to age 65 in the year 2000 could expect to live 15.9 years more. A woman who had lived to age 65 in 1940 could expect to live an average of 13.4 years more. But a woman who had lived to age 65 in the year 2000 could expect to live an average of 19.2 years more.

And the final two lines of the above tabulation show that the Social Security actuaries' best ("intermediate") estimate of life expectancies in the year 2075 is that our lives will continue to be even longer.

So, in the time from when Social Security began (1940) until now (2001), our life expectancies have gone up by 12 to 14 years. And they are estimated to go up by another 6 to 7 years by the year 2075. Yet, we still have a Social Security benefit schedule that starts paying at the same age 62 (for 20% less benefits) or at the same age 65 (for full benefits). We're living much longer, but the benefits still start paying at age 62–65.

Another point that needs to be made is about the different life expectancies of blacks. U.S. black males born in 1996 have a life expectancy of just over 66 years. U.S. black females born in 1996 have a life expectancy of just over 74 years. Both of these expectancies are of course less than for whites, but for black males the difference is the greatest.

That means that they have a much lower chance of ever

collecting Social Security retirement benefits. And it also means that it would very likely be to their benefit that they be saving money in their own retirement accounts (where the money will always accumulate for them or their heirs) instead of paying a large part of their income into a federal retirement plan from which they will most likely never collect.

In 1983, the decision was made (as part of a major plan to try to rescue Social Security from its serious financial problems then) to raise the normal retirement date gradually from 65 to 67. The change from a normal retirement date (full benefits) at 65 to 67 starts taking effect in the year 2003. And the normal retirement age gradually raises now until it is 67 in the year 2025.

Early retirement had meant that if you retired one year early, benefits were cut by 6 2/3%. If you retired two years early, the cut was 13 1/3%. If you retired three years early, the cut was 20%. Now that was increased to be that if you retired four years early (but still not before age 62), the cut was 25%, and if you retired five years early (but still not before age 62), the cut was 30%.

(The whole schedule of new normal retirement ages (NRAs), as they now stand, shows in column 3 of Table 14-1 on page 248.)

Before we move on...

We need to stop long enough to review that you are absorbing all of this information, in this case about Social Security. You are up-to-speed at this point if you understand:

> ...how the "trustees" of the Social Security funds are not truly independent.

...how they have no real options as to where they are to invest their funds or whether those to whom they loan their money are creditworthy or can really pay it back.

...how the Social Security "trustees" do not function the way most of us think "trustees" have responsibilities.

...how, for all practical purposes, there *is* no trust fund. It has no money in it. All it has in it is IOUs from Congress.

...that a "special Treasury bond" isn't a "bond" as you would normally think of it. Those are words meaning, "an IOU from Congress."

...that "interest income" for the Social Security fund is in truth just a further obligation by Congress, which is putting its interest expense obligations "on the tab."

...how artificially raising the interest rate that Social Security charges Congress is just accounting and solves nothing.

... that the "FICA" tax that you pay is a payroll tax (not a "contribution") and it doesn't buy you "insurance," regardless of what the letters FICA stand for.

...that you pay income tax on those amounts that you pay as payroll taxes.

...that what you pay into Social Security has essentially no relationship to what you may get out as benefits, because what you put in is not for you.

...that some of us (with lower working incomes) get paid

higher retirement benefits, compared to our incomes, than others.

...that you don't have money sitting in some account with your name and number on it, just for you.

...that you aren't "guaranteed" any benefits. (The U.S. Supreme Court has said so).

...what "pay-as-you-go" means.

...how if you die before reaching retirement, you would receive no benefits at all from Social Security (although your survivors might), but how if you had been putting that money into a real savings account of your own (instead of paying payroll taxes) you *would* leave that money in a real account of your own.

...about the SSI Supplemental Security Income program, about how it is something quite separate from Social Security, and how it would continue to be available as retirement income protection for those in need.

...what the assurances about "the year 2037" really mean.

...the difference between "optimistic," "intermediate," and "pessimistic" projections, and who it is who makes these projections.

...the 4 sources of income to the Social Security OASDI funds.

...the difference between cash income (two sources) and

"not real cash" income (two other possible sources).

...what has to happen to ever turn that "not real cash" income into being real "cash income" out of which Social Security can pay retirement benefits.

...the date by which (according to the "intermediate" forecast) these trust funds will have more cash outgo than they have cash income.

...the date by which (according to the "pessimistic" forecast) these trust funds will have more cash outgo than they have cash income.

...where the money would actually have to come from, if the U.S. government is going to be able to pay back to the Social Security funds what it owes them.

...where that money will come from, eventually, if the U.S. government decides to borrow it from the public for now and pay it back to the public later.

...what the shortfall will be *per year* in the year 2038, even if the U.S. government *has* paid Social Security everything it owes it.

...whether the situation then gets even better or even worse.

...what the payroll tax rate will have to be by the year 2037, or by the year 2075, in order to cover the expected shortfall.

...how many trillions and hundreds of billions of dollars the shortfall is expected to be *each year* by the year 2040, according to the pessimistic forecast.

...how many trillions and hundreds of billions of dollars the shortfall is expected to be *each year* by the year 2075, according to the pessimistic forecast, and how that will be more than twice the amount of money coming in each year.

...how it would take payroll tax rates of over 28% of taxable income to cover these obligations by then, with the situation getting worse and the rates going up.

...how accurate the actuaries are able to be, given that they are doing the best job possible of predicting the future.

...how the Social Security actuaries in 1989 predicted 7 major factors for the year 2000, and on how many of those 7 factors the actual results turned out to be outside the range (of "optimistic" or "pessimistic") that they had forecast.

...how the forecasts of the year in which these trust funds would be "exhausted" have kept changing.

...why the actuaries expect the growth of the economy (GDP) to slow.

...what the forecast is for the U.S. total fertility rate, and how that compares to the other developed countries of the world.

...how a U.S. total fertility rate lower than the forecast made by the actuaries would result in lower payroll tax income.

...how increases in life expectancy, greater than the forecast of the actuaries, would increase the payouts that the

Social Security funds have to make.

...what life expectancy was for the average male or female in the U.S. back in 1940 (when Social Security began paying benefits).

...what it is now, and what it is expected to be by the year 2075.

...therefore, the number of additional years that we can expect to live, compared to when the Social Security benefits were originally established (to start paying at ages 62 and 65).

...how different life expectancies are for blacks, and particularly for black males, and how that translates into less Social Security retirement benefits for them.

...how the normal retirement dates, at which Social Security starts paying benefits, are being increased, on what schedule, and with what effect on the reduction of benefits for those who choose to retire early.

...that, to say the very least, the future of Social Security has risks of its own.

For those of you interested in doing further reading about Social Security, these are some of the best references:

The Annual Reports of the Board of Trustees of the Old-Age and Survivors Insurance and Disability Insurance Trust Funds, available at no charge from the Social Security Administration, phone: 1-800-772-1213.

Ziggy

> IN OTHER NEWS... THE SOCIAL SECURITY FUND WAS STABILIZED, CONGRESS BALANCED THE BUDGET, AND HELL FROZE OVER!

Ziggy ©Ziggy and Friends Inc.
Reprinted with permission of Universal Press Syndicate. All rights reserved.

The Real Deal: The History and Future of Social Security, by Sylvester J. Schieber and John B. Shoven. 1999

Social Security – The Inherent Contradiction, by Peter J. Ferrara, 1980

www.ssa.gov (the website of the Social Security Administration)

When you have all of that down pat, (and maybe have taken a little time to recover), then you are ready to move on and consider at least a few of the facts about investment and so-called "privatization."

Question #8

What Are the Facts about Investment and "Privatization"?

Investment

For some people, it may be scary to think of leaving Social "Security" and to consider "investing," when they haven't invested before or maybe have some antagonistic attitudes toward "Wall Street" or even toward "management." These people may have had a little extra money in a CD, but haven't bought or wouldn't buy stocks. For these people, "investment" would be a risky venture into the unknown.

The good news for them is that these fears can be addressed at least a couple ways. The first way is to narrow the problem down to just those few things that a new investor would really need to know (if electing to leave Social Security and instead to put the money into a privately-owned account). The second way to then address these fears is to learn a few basic facts. Turn it from fear of the unknown to being faith in the known.

First, to narrow the problem down, we can probably estimate that few of us 45 or older will be considering the "privatization" alternative unless we already are knowledgeable about investment. The problem will be one for mainly the younger generations to consider.

Fortunately, IRAs (Individual Retirement Accounts) have now

been around for more than 25 years, 401(k)s (for similar tax-deferred saving) have been used now for nearly 20 years, 50% of households own mutual funds, and 20% of families have direct stock holdings. So it isn't as if this subject of investment is totally new to everyone.

Beyond that, in order to elect "privatization," you don't have to have a stock broker, you don't need to pick individual stocks, you don't need to worry about whether "the market" is going up or down, and there is no need for you to be worrying about the frantic ups and downs of whatever category of stocks (biotech? telecom? dot.com?) is "hot" at the moment (or cold the next).

Instead, there are basically ten general things that you *do* need to know:

The difference between "spending" and "investment"

#1. The difference between "spending" and "investment." When you spend money, you get something for it at that time. When, on the other hand, you invest, that investment (whether it be in a CD (certificate of deposit), a bond, a stock, or real estate) is expected to hold its value, increase its value, and pay you back. The payback is often on a regular basis, such as monthly interest income to you or quarterly dividends on a stock.

Money presently taken out of your pay as payroll taxes is either spent immediately for someone else's retirement benefits or is loaned by the Social Security Administration to the U.S. government, where Congress *spends* it. In either case, it gets spent.

If, on the other hand, you put your money into bonds or stocks, you do that with a definite expectation of a payback of money, called a "return on investment." If you put $1,000 in an account at the beginning of the year, for example, and at the end of the year that $1,000 has grown (by having interest income) by $100, to become $1,100, you have had a one year 10% return on investment.

This distinction between spending and investment is *extremely* important for you to understand, because it is the basic difference between a government-based retirement income plan and a private investment-based plan.

In the government-based plan (such as Social Security), the money is *not* invested over the years so it can be earning. Instead, if any money is collected before it is needed, it is simply *spent* (on something else). With a private investment-based plan, the money that is saved is actually put into something (typically a business) that really *earns money, AND allows you to compound those earnings over the years..*

If you study *any* privatization plan, meant to solve the problems of the present Social Security plan, what the plan is inevitably trying to do is to somehow get money set aside and *invested over time.* Whether that investment is to be done partly or entirely by the government, or is to be part of a mixed government/private plan, you will find that the part that is going to make the difference is the part that is *invested.* That is because the invested money *grows and compounds*, whereas money collected in taxes and then paid out is simply a one-for-one transfer of a non-growing amount.

Everyone knows that "pay-as-you-go" won't work. The solution has to be to get the money set aside and growing in value because it is *invested.*

Don't forget that, regardless of what plan you are looking at, the more that the money that is put into it is invested (in profit-making assets), the more it is going to grow in value. If only 2% is invested, for example, you can figure that the plan will *not* provide much growth in the amount that is put into it.

JUST FOR FUN

"It's a relaxation tape — the sound of interest accruing."

The power of compounding

#2. The power of "compound interest" or of compounded return on investment. You absolutely *have* to understand this, in order to plan for your later years. The sooner in your life you understand compounding, the better.

In the above example, in which the $1,000 became $1,100 in a year, let's look at two possibilities. The first is that you take out the $100 gain, spend it, and then start the second year with the original $1,000. You are now continuing to earn *simple* interest. The second possibility is, instead, *compound* interest: you leave the $1,100 in the account so that not only the original $1,000 continues to earn interest, but the $100 stays and *also* starts earning interest income. This way, you are also earning with what you have earned.

What Are the Facts about Investment and "Privatization"? 131

It is sometimes said that you can make money two ways: by working, and by having your money working.

We will give you more examples of compound interest or compounded return on investment, because of its importance in your financial planning, but will first illustrate it with a simple rule:

The "Rule of 72"

#3. The "rule of 72." This rule is not completely accurate, but it is close enough to give you the general picture about the power of compounding. The rule tells you how many years it takes you to double your money.

The number 72 is what you get by multiplying (1) a rate of return (such as 10% per year) times (2) the number of years that you reinvest your money and compound that return.

For example, if you earn 6% on your money, compounded, you will double that money in 12 years. 6% x 12 years = 72.

Or if you earn 12% on your money, compounded, you will double your money in 6 years. 12% x 6 years = 72.

But let's take that last example forward for *another* six years. The $1,000 became $2,000 in 6 years. Now you continue to invest for 6 more years with a 12% average annual return. The $2,000 now becomes $4,000. And in 6 *more* years the $4,000 becomes $8,000.

In 18 years, the $1,000 becomes $8,000. This is compounding at work.

As you start thinking of that money doubling and doubling (8 – 16 – 32 – 64), you understand the importance of starting early and having time for compounding to work to your advantage.

But it is even better than that. We have been talking about one amount of money put into an investment once. There is of course the additional opportunity to keep putting money into savings monthly and yearly throughout your life. We'll get into some examples of how amazing the result can be, but let's start with some simple examples.

We do need to repeat that we are talking about "tax deferred" earnings. In other words, there is no tax on the amount earned during the year in which it is earned. Instead, that earned amount can be reinvested. The tax is deferred. You do not have to pay it until some day in the future at which time you decide to spend the money.

If you start saving at the age of 20, planning to retire at 70, you have 50 years in which to compound your returns. To start with, let's look simply at $10,000 invested one time at age 20, and what it can earn in a given number of years at various average annual returns on investment:

	In 10 yrs.	In 20 yrs.	In 30 yrs.	In 40 yrs.	In 50 yrs.
At 6%	$17,908	$32,071	$ 57,435	$102,857	$ 184,202
At 8%	$21,589	$46,610	$100,626	$217,245	$ 469,016
At 10%	$25,937	$67,275	$174,494	$452,593	$1,173,909
At 12%	$31,058	$96,463	$299,599	$930,510	$2,890,022

All of this from investing $10,000 once. Notice the double-whammy effect of not only the years but of earning just 2% more per year over that time.

(Later on, we'll look at what the odds are that you can earn those rates of return, but for now the important thing is that you understand compounding.)

But now let's look at what the results would be on just these assumptions: you start with nothing saved, but starting at age 20 you put $2,000 per year into savings (as a regular monthly set-aside of $166.67), and those saved amounts earn at those same rates over the same number of years:

	In 10 Yrs.	In 20 Yrs.	In 30 Yrs.	In 40 Yrs.	In 50 Yrs.
At 6%	$27,079	$ 75,575	$162,422	$ 317,953	$ 596,484
At 8%	$30,021	$ 94,835	$234,763	$ 536,857	$1,189,056
At 10%	$33,311	$119,712	$343,814	$ 925,077	$2,432,722
At 12%	$36,989	$151,872	$508,679	$1,616,869	$5,058,739

If a husband and wife would together be putting aside $4,000/year, then the above numbers would of course be doubled.

Or, of course, if you were, for example, starting at age 40 and wondering what the results could be in the 30 years until you are 70, you can look in the "In 30 years" column above, etc.

(If you want to do further calculations of this sort yourself, you can do them on standard computer programs such as Microsoft Money/PlanningWizards/Savings Calculator).

One of the more fascinating examples of the power of compounding was published by The Institute for Econometric Research in 1993 in its "Market Logic." Their "Early Start IRA: How $6,750 Grows to Over $1 Million" is shown on page 134. In all cases, they are assuming compounded growth in value at an annual rate of 10%.

The importance of getting started early is shown in their examples of Investors B, C, and D, each of whom accumulated around a million dollars in a lifetime by investing (respectively) a total of only $14,000, or $10,000, or $6,750.

Average returns on investment in large stocks

#4. The fourth thing you do need to know is what average returns on investment in large stocks have been over the years. The most famous source for this information is Ibbotson Asociates of Chicago, which publishes an annual Yearbook,

Early Start IRA: How $6,750 Grows To Over $1 Million

This table shows four ways to accumulate approximately $1,000,000 in an IRA by age 65 at 10% a year compounded. Investor A contributes $2,000 at the beginning of each year for forty years (ages 26-65); Investor B, $2,000 a year for only seven years (19-25); Investor C, $2,000 a year for only five years (age 14-18); and Investor D smaller sums still from age 8 through 13. Finally, Investor E shows the IRA growth achieved by making all of these contributions at every age from 8 to 65.

Age	INVESTOR A Contribution	INVESTOR A Year-End Value	INVESTOR B Contribution	INVESTOR B Year-End Value	INVESTOR C Contribution	INVESTOR C Year-End Value	INVESTOR D Contribution	INVESTOR D Year-End Value	INVESTOR E Contribution	INVESTOR E Year-End Value
8	-0-	-0-	-0-	-0-	-0-	-0-	500	550	500	550
9	-0-	-0-	-0-	-0-	-0-	-0-	750	1,430	750	1,430
10	-0-	-0-	-0-	-0-	-0-	-0-	1,000	2,673	1,000	2,673
11	-0-	-0-	-0-	-0-	-0-	-0-	1,250	4,315	1,250	4,315
12	-0-	-0-	-0-	-0-	-0-	-0-	1,500	6,397	1,500	6,397
13	-0-	-0-	-0-	-0-	-0-	-0-	1,750	8,962	1,750	8,962
14	-0-	-0-	-0-	-0-	2,000	2,200	-0-	9,858	2,000	12,058
15	-0-	-0-	-0-	-0-	2,000	4,620	-0-	10,843	2,000	15,463
16	-0-	-0-	-0-	-0-	2,000	7,282	-0-	11,928	2,000	19,210
17	-0-	-0-	-0-	-0-	2,000	10,210	-0-	13,121	2,000	23,331
18	-0-	-0-	-0-	-0-	2,000	13,431	-0-	14,433	2,000	27,864
19	-0-	-0-	2,000	2,200	-0-	14,774	-0-	15,876	2,000	32,850
20	-0-	-0-	2,000	4,620	-0-	16,252	-0-	17,463	2,000	38,335
21	-0-	-0-	2,000	7,282	-0-	17,877	-0-	19,210	2,000	44,369
22	-0-	-0-	2,000	10,210	-0-	19,665	-0-	21,131	2,000	51,006
23	-0-	-0-	2,000	13,431	-0-	21,631	-0-	23,244	2,000	58,306
24	-0-	-0-	2,000	16,974	-0-	23,794	-0-	25,568	2,000	66,337
25	-0-	-0-	2,000	20,872	-0-	26,174	-0-	28,125	2,000	75,170
26	2,000	2,200	-0-	22,959	-0-	28,791	-0-	30,938	2,000	84,888
27	2,000	4,620	-0-	25,255	-0-	31,670	-0-	34,031	2,000	95,576
28	2,000	7,282	-0-	27,780	-0-	34,837	-0-	37,434	2,000	107,334
29	2,000	10,210	-0-	30,558	-0-	38,321	-0-	41,178	2,000	120,267
30	2,000	13,431	-0-	33,614	-0-	42,153	-0-	45,296	2,000	134,494
31	2,000	16,974	-0-	36,976	-0-	46,368	-0-	49,825	2,000	150,143
32	2,000	20,872	-0-	40,673	-0-	51,005	-0-	54,808	2,000	167,358
33	2,000	25,159	-0-	44,741	-0-	56,106	-0-	60,289	2,000	186,294
34	2,000	29,875	-0-	49,215	-0-	61,716	-0-	66,317	2,000	207,123
35	2,000	35,062	-0-	54,136	-0-	67,888	-0-	72,949	2,000	230,035
36	2,000	40,769	-0-	59,550	-0-	74,676	-0-	80,244	2,000	255,239
37	2,000	47,045	-0-	65,505	-0-	82,144	-0-	88,269	2,000	282,963
38	2,000	53,950	-0-	72,055	-0-	90,359	-0-	97,095	2,000	313,459
39	2,000	61,545	-0-	79,261	-0-	99,394	-0-	106,805	2,000	347,005
40	2,000	69,899	-0-	87,187	-0-	109,334	-0-	117,485	2,000	383,905
41	2,000	79,089	-0-	95,905	-0-	120,267	-0-	129,234	2,000	424,496
42	2,000	89,198	-0-	105,496	-0-	132,294	-0-	142,157	2,000	469,145
43	2,000	100,318	-0-	116,045	-0-	145,523	-0-	156,373	2,000	518,269
44	2,000	112,550	-0-	127,650	-0-	160,076	-0-	172,010	2,000	572,286
45	2,000	126,005	-0-	140,415	-0-	176,083	-0-	189,211	2,000	631,714
46	2,000	140,805	-0-	154,456	-0-	193,692	-0-	208,133	2,000	697,086
47	2,000	157,086	-0-	169,902	-0-	213,061	-0-	228,946	2,000	768,995
48	2,000	174,995	-0-	186,892	-0-	234,367	-0-	251,840	2,000	848,094
49	2,000	194,694	-0-	205,581	-0-	257,803	-0-	277,024	2,000	935,103
50	2,000	216,364	-0-	226,140	-0-	283,358	-0-	304,727	2,000	1,030,814
51	2,000	240,200	-0-	248,754	-0-	311,942	-0-	335,209	2,000	1,136,095
52	2,000	266,420	-0-	273,629	-0-	343,136	-0-	368,719	2,000	1,251,905
53	2,000	295,262	-0-	300,992	-0-	377,450	-0-	405,591	2,000	1,379,295
54	2,000	326,988	-0-	331,091	-0-	415,195	-0-	446,150	2,000	1,519,425
55	2,000	361,887	-0-	364,200	-0-	456,715	-0-	490,766	2,000	1,673,567
56	2,000	400,276	-0-	400,620	-0-	502,386	-0-	539,842	2,000	1,843,124
57	2,000	442,503	-0-	440,682	-0-	552,625	-0-	593,826	2,000	2,029,636
58	2,000	488,953	-0-	484,750	-0-	607,887	-0-	653,209	2,000	2,234,800
59	2,000	540,049	-0-	533,225	-0-	668,676	-0-	718,530	2,000	2,460,480
60	2,000	596,254	-0-	586,548	-0-	735,543	-0-	790,383	2,000	2,708,728
61	2,000	658,079	-0-	645,203	-0-	809,098	-0-	869,421	2,000	2,981,800
62	2,000	726,087	-0-	709,723	-0-	890,007	-0-	956,363	2,000	3,282,180
63	2,000	800,896	-0-	780,695	-0-	979,008	-0-	1,052,000	2,000	3,612,598
64	2,000	883,185	-0-	858,765	-0-	1,076,909	-0-	1,157,200	2,000	3,976,058
65	2,000	973,704	-0-	944,641	-0-	1,184,600	-0-	1,272,930	2,000	4,375,864
Less Total Invested:		(80,000)		(14,000)		(10,000)		(6,750)		(110,750)
Equals Net Earnings:		893,704		930,641		1,174,600		1,266,170		4,265,114
Money Grew:		11-fold		66-fold		117-fold		188-fold		38-fold

"Stocks, Bonds, Bills and Inflation," updating data that they have compiled since 1926. One group of stocks that they follow is "large company stocks," which are now represented by the Standard and Poors 500, which is a group of 500 of the largest stocks that represent all parts of the U.S. economy and which is the most commonly-used measurement of the general stock market.

Over nearly 75 years, the annual return on these large company stocks has averaged nearly 11%. That return is made up of the dividends paid on these stocks plus the amount by which the stocks went up in price.

Some pessimistic economists expect that, if the growth of the economy (GDP) in the U.S. is going to slow down, that means that the potential growth of profits (that are the basis of the growth of stock prices) would have to slow down too. So stock prices couldn't keep going up as they have. They are forgetting that U.S. businesses are of course involved in trade with other countries. They also forget that the United States is only one part of the world economy, that many parts of the world are coming from behind and therefore growing much faster than the United States, and that there are profits to be made by investment outside the United States.

The market does not go up every year!

#5. The fifth thing you need to be aware of, though, is that the market does not go up 11% every year. In fact, it doesn't even go up every year. Some entire years, the market goes down. The market, even as an average of many, many individual stocks, bounces around daily, monthly, quarterly, annually. But the important point is how it averages out over the long haul.

When you consider saving money for retirement, you are definitely talking about the long haul, and not about what happened to some temporarily-hot stocks last week. So it is important to invest for the long haul and to look, not for short-term results, but for long-term results. That means accepting short-term ups and downs. You might say that the road isn't straight as an arrow, but it does get you there.

One year that is mentioned often as an example of what can happen in the market was 1987. That year, the market suddenly dropped 22% in one day. What people usually don't mention is that the market nevertheless by year end was up 5% from where it had started on January 1.

Stocks (or "shares" of stock) are part ownership of a company, and over the long run, stock prices will go up in line with the profits (or "earnings") of the companies. At times, the market will be more optimistic and will pay higher prices, in reference to those earnings. Stocks will then be at higher "P/E" ratios, meaning higher price/earnings ratios. At other times, the people buying and selling stocks will be more pessimistic, and there will be lower P/E ratios. But you are interested in the long haul, which will average these things out.

The important thing for you to understand in summary is that the longer you hold stocks (or a mutual fund, that in turn owns many stocks), the less fluctuation you will have in your average annual % return. For example, if you look at the record all the way back to 1926 for individual years, the market may have – in any one year — gone up more than 50% or down more than 40%. But if you look at any 25 years in a row, the range drops to being a high return – for any 25 years — averaging 15% a year or a low return averaging 6% per year.

It would be quite irrational, for example, to have the national discussion of Social Security and potential privatization be influenced much, one way or another, by how the market is doing at that particular moment. Some people could say, "This down market just shows the dangers of investing." People who had a longer-range understanding of the market would, on the other hand, need to assure them that, yes, the market doesn't always go up. It does go up and down, but over time it always goes up.

The value of investing regularly

#6. The sixth thing to know is the value of investing regularly at a steady rate. This is known as "dollar-cost averaging," meaning that you average out the cost of what you buy by not trying to "buy low" and "sell high," but simply by buying regularly, even as the market goes up and down.

The opposite of regular purchases is trying to "play the market" or "time the market," and that simply doesn't work, particularly for amateurs and certainly not for everyone who has money invested for retirement. Many, many studies of market history have shown that market "timing" (of purchases and sales) simply does not work, largely because the market makes major moves only at certain times. Even the experts find that they miss those major, sudden and unpredictable moves if they are not in the market then.

So you don't need to be worrying about buying and selling. Your purchases are "buy and hold," and history has shown that steady, regular purchases are the way to win. That way, you miss the excitement of gambling, but you enjoy the gains of patience and persistence.

The right kinds of mutual funds

#7. You of course need to know not only what a "mutual fund" is, but what "index funds," "diversified funds," "balanced funds," "equity-income funds," and "large cap funds" are. The general point to know about all of these is that you do not want all your eggs in one basket. You want to spread the risk and stay away from risk as much as possible. You want to stay in the middle of the road.

Accordingly, you do not want to be investing in funds or stocks that specialize in just one industry or one kind of business, such as pharmaceutical stocks. You may want to invest in these specialized "sector" or "select" funds with other money, but not with your basic retirement funds.

Rather than buy individual stocks or bonds, you can buy shares in a "mutual fund," and that mutual fund then buys a lot of stocks and/or bonds for you. There are all kinds of mutual funds, depending on what kinds of stocks or bonds you want to be invested in. Some mutual funds pick risky situations and go for higher returns. In the case of your retirement funds, you want a low-risk mutual fund, but one that will not be so low-risk that there is an inadequate return. That is going to mean that you want to invest through a mutual fund that invests in stocks, or in a combination of stocks and bonds.

The diversified funds buy in many industries or parts of the economy, for the specific purpose of spreading risk. The term "large cap" means large capitalization, with capitalization being the total value of the stock in that company. So these are the largest companies, and generally therefore the safest ones. Funds that invest in both stocks and bonds are generally known as either "balanced" funds or "equity-income" funds (the "equity" referring to the stocks and the "income" referring to the bonds).

Finally, there are "index" funds. There are several of these, and each one of them is meant to be a specific group of stocks that represent some aspect of the market. There may be an index fund of European stocks, or emerging market stocks, of small cap stocks, or international stocks. But what you would be looking for is an index fund that covers a large group of diversified large companies. The most typical index is of the Standard & Poors 500 stocks.

In any case, these are the types of mutual funds in which you will want to have your funds invested for the long haul, toward providing yourself with a retirement income. Other investment is another story, and isn't something that we're getting into here.

How low the charges on a mutual fund will be

#8. You may wonder whether you have to pay too much to have someone do all of this investing for you. This is in fact something to watch, because the fees that the mutual funds charge come right out of the annual earnings of the money you have invested in that fund.

The larger the fund, probably the less it will charge (as a percentage of what you have invested). If you are buying the fund through your company, these charges may be less. The number you are looking for is the "expense ratio."

For the kind of fund that you are looking for, this expense ratio (or charge to you for management of your money) should be less than 1.0% per year. In the case of the large Vanguard 500 Index Fund, the charge is usually around .18% to .20%. That is l/5 of one percent or less, or a total charge of about $180 to $200 per year for management of $100,000. With an index fund, the managers do not have to do a lot of analytical work; they simply buy the stocks that make up that index.

The TIAA-CREF fund (Teachers Insurance and Annuity Association – College Retirement Equities Fund) is the main retirement system for the nation's colleges and universities. Their 11 funds have expense ratios ranging from a high of 49/100 of 1% (for the international stock fund) to a low of 26/100 of 1% (for the equity index fund), with the median fund costing 30/100 of 1% of assets.

The federal government employees' TSP (Thrift Savings

Plan) has an expense ratio of 9/10 of 1%.

In general, the more money that these funds manage, the lower these expense ratios will go.

"Defined benefit" vs. "Defined contribution" plans

#9. You need to be aware of the general concepts of "defined benefit" plans and "defined contribution" retirement plans, because the trend is definitely away from the one and to the other.

The pension plan that used to be typical in a large manufacturing company was a "defined benefit" plan. It was defined, or spelled out, as to what benefit you would receive when you retired. That benefit was possible, first, because Congress gave the company a tax advantage. The company could call the amount that it put away for the retirement fund a taxable deductible expense. But if the company put that same amount in the workers' paychecks (so the workers could invest in their own retirement savings plans), it was taxable income to the workers, leaving them only after-tax money to invest.

So the company, instead of putting the money into the workers' paychecks, set the money aside in a pension plan, based on total payroll each year. But some of those employees left the company or died before retiring, and only those who stuck with the one company until they retired actually collected the retirement income. With so few collecting, it was possible to pay a decent benefit.

However, the U.S. workforce has gotten more mobile, moving from job to job during a lifetime, but still wanting to save for retirement. Additionally, the laws and accounting on "defined benefit" programs got more and more difficult for companies to deal with.

The IRAs and 401(k) plans came along to fill this need for personal control and portability *and* to give the workers the same

What Are the Facts about Investment and "Privatization"? 141

tax advantage that only the companies had had before. But these plans do not define the benefit. They define only the "contribution." These are "defined contribution" plans. In other words, they are not promising what the *outcome*, the benefit at retirement time, will be. They can only commit as to (1) what will be put *into* the retirement fund and (2) what investment choices you have.

So the traditional "defined benefit" plan is fast becoming a thing of the past. Plans today have "portability," meaning that the retirement funds that you build up in one company can then be moved to the next company or into your own account. And, for the first time, they give the tax advantage to people themselves.

Another way to look at "defined benefit" plans versus "defined contribution" plans is that the party that takes the risk gets the reward. With the defined benefit plan, it is the company or the government taking the risk (that they will be able to provide the promised benefit). So they have to hedge that bet, and be sure they don't promise (or give) too much. In the case of the old-style company pension plan, there is a lot of calculation done as to how many workers actually won't be around to collect, what rate of return can be made on the invested funds, how many will retire and live how long, etc. But the money is at least actually invested and earning. In the case of Social Security, which is also a defined benefit plan, the money is of course not invested, but the actuaries are in this case looking ahead and seeing that they are not going to be able to deliver on what Congress has already promised.

In the defined benefit plan, it is the company or government taking the basic risk, with the worker's secondary risk being only that the company or government won't deliver. The company plans (and the plans covering the retirement income of members of Congress) are accordingly kept safe by very strict government regulation. But the only regulation on the Social

Security plan is by Congress.

In the defined *contribution* plan, however, it is the contributor who is taking the risk. Whatever return there is, it will all belong to the contributor. The risk belongs to the contributor, so that is scary and uncertain for people used to having others be responsible for or look out for them.

This becomes a major philosophical debate when Social Security and privatization are examined, because there is this question of who is taking what risk. For now, just realize that there is risk for the worker in *either* plan (as just covered in the last two paragraphs).

In the last few decades, retirement income planning has become more the responsibility of each one of us, rather than the responsibility of our employers and the government. Stop and think about this. It has happened for one major reason. Congress passed laws (for IRAs and 401ks) that took away the tax penalties they had previously applied to personal retirement savings.

We need to recognize that there is in fact a paternalism, an "I need to take care of them" attitude, implicit in many of the Social Security reform plans. Let's not call that a criticism, but let's realize that this attitude, this approach exists. And to some degree, it is of course justified.

But we also need to recognize a similar desire on the part of many, if not of most of us, to be able to take care of these things ourselves – if given half a chance by our tax system.

It is appropriate to point out how the existence of the mandatory defined-benefit Social Security program has lifted, in particular, many elderly women out of what would otherwise have been poverty. But another couple points can also be made. One is that a large part of the improvement for those women came from a greatly improved economy and standard of living in the United States over the last few decades. And the other point is to ask how much better off these women might have been if

What Are the Facts about Investment and "Privatization"? 143

they had been required to put the same amount of money all those years, not into Social Security, but into an invested private account of the kind being discussed now.

In some ways, the two schools of thought may be that, on the one hand "we need to take care of everybody," and on the other hand, "no, we need to be able to take care of ourselves."

If our government, by its taxation and withholding of 10.6% of our salaries or wages, before we even get them, takes that responsibility away from us (or makes it financially impractical), the second school of thought (personal responsibility) doesn't get a chance.

When Congress first gave tax deferral status to IRAs, the surge of savings was so large that Congress had to immediately back off. People were saving *too much!* This meant that Congress wasn't getting the income tax that it needed! So guess what took priority? Taxes were immediately voted back in, to make sure that people didn't do too much saving on their own. To this day, Congress is afraid to take much taxation off IRAs, because they know people will (show personal responsibility and) take maximum advantage of it.

Bottom line: when reviewing various proposals related to Social Security, we need to be aware of where each plan fits on the spectrum of government responsibility versus personal responsibility. Defined contribution plans are personal responsibility plans.

The safety that government regulation will provide

#10. Finally, you can be sure that the government will put restrictions on as to what investments can be made, with what mutual funds or other financial organizations. With such an important national program, and with the obvious expectation that many people simply will not be financially sophisticated, the rules and regulations will undoubtedly be not only similar to those that have already worked for IRAs and 401(k) plans, but even more strict. The object in all cases will be to make these plans as safe as possible.

So, in summary, all you need to know about "investment" in order to start funding your own retirement savings plan is those ten general principles or facts. And now you *do* know them. Understanding those things, you'll stay in the middle of the road and take advantage of the proven historical advantages of the compounding power of money that is not spent but is reinvested over the long term.

For those who would want to look into the subject of investment a little more, as you think about privatization, these are some of the best books:

Bogle on Mutual Funds, by John C. Bogle, 1994.

The Motley Fool Investment Guide; How the Fool Beats Wall Street's Wise Men and How You Can Too (Updated), by David and Tom Gardner, 2001

The Only Investment Guide You'll Ever Need (Updated), by Andrew P. Tobias, 1999

With this basic knowledge about investment, you can then look at what would probably be the general program for "privatization."

Privatization

The term "privatization," if people accept it totally as an alternative to the present Social Security retirement plan, refers to those people (1) electing to no longer have payroll taxes deducted from their paychecks for retirement income purposes (that amount currently being 5.30% of taxable payroll), (2) agreeing to not expect to receive any retirement income from Social Security, and (3) instead getting tax deferral status for money they set aside in personal government-approved retirement funds of their own.

In other words, people electing complete privatization would no longer be giving the 5.30% of their income to Social Security (in expectation that Social Security might provide a minimum retirement income), but would instead be taking advantage of tax deferral provisions that allow them to do their own investing and retirement income saving.

So why is "privatization" even being considered? One reason is of course that it makes it possible for money to be set aside so it actually *earns* more money. That is what Social Security does *not* do.

But there is another reason that you have to keep in mind at all times, when asking whether a particular privatization plan gets the job done. That reason is that the Social Security retirement plan, as it is now set up, has an enormous, future obligation to make payments *that it cannot make*.

So get this very clear: the object of getting people to elect privatization is to get people off of Social Security so that they are no longer a part of that enormous present impossible future liability.

If people are given incentives to save, that is of course good. But it is more important that, in exchange for receiving those incentives (of tax deferral), they agree to no longer be a part of that future liability of the Social Security plan. It has to be a tradeoff. The object is to remove that impossible future liability of the present Social Security system. So if people are given the chance to save 2% of their income (tax-deferred, like an IRA), on top of (or in addition to) the Social Security plan, that isn't going to get rid of the future liabilities of the plan. Or if people are offered 2% in exchange for giving up some benefits, and don't consider that enough incentive to switch, then the objective isn't accomplished. Or if they <u>do</u> accept a 2% plan and get a fair tradeoff, as we will see later, that isn't going to be enough to get rid of the liability and accomplish the objective either.

Beyond that, remember that any "2%" plan isn't going to get the job done, so it thereby means that Social Security will both (1) remain mainly a defined-benefit plan and (2) continue to have its future liabilities.

If the objective is really to eliminate that future liability, plain and simple, *2% isn't going to hack it.*

The cleanest solution is a plan that gives as many workers as possible enough incentive to get *completely* out of Social Security retirement plan <u>and</u> that therefore removes those workers from the future liabilities of the Social Security plan. Also, as we'll see, the timing right now is perfect for getting the job done with real answers. The alternative is to pussyfoot with compromise solutions that let the window of opportunity close and that therefore pass this problem on to our children and grandchildren.

If we don't solve this problem in a big way right now, too many workers remain on the Social Security retirement plan and the future liabilities of that plan —the problem we are trying to solve — also remain. And the opportunity to have solved the problem is lost.

So the impossible future liabilities of the Social Security retirement plan are the problem, and the way to remove those liabilities is to give enough incentives to as many workers as possible so they will elect to leave the plan. Those incentives have to be good enough that people will decide that they can do better on their own. And if they don't decide that, then they can stay with the present plan.

That of course means that we have to look at what the <u>cost</u>

of those incentives (to get people to leave the Social Security retirement plan) would be, as compared to the expected future cost of all those liabilities of the plan. The cost has to (1) be enough to be a real incentive for people to leave the Social Security retirement plan, (2) in return, remove an offsetting future liability of that plan, (3) be a good deal for all of us and something we can afford to pay (in the form of "transition costs"), and (4) be paid in a way that assures that the money will still be there for those who are already on the Social Security retirement plan or who still want to go on that plan.

In all discussions of privatization, then, the first point that always needs to be made is that it would not, it must not, significantly change or affect the benefits being received by present retirees, or the benefits that are to be received by those who are still working and who are too close to retirement to be able to be making any changes.

In truth, that group of retirees or near-retirees is already in far more danger than they probably realize of not having enough payroll taxes coming in to pay what they expect as benefits. That group actually needs to question whether privatization (and the changes that would go with it) would be bad for or maybe even *good* for them. The Social Security retirement income program is in fact in deep trouble, and the retirees and near-retirees need to consider privatization as a possible answer, not as something to which they have a thoughtless knee-jerk opposition. They will really be lucky if the changes make it possible for them to just get essentially what they presently expect as retirement benefits.

But, given that necessary starting declaration, we also need to spell out what privatization would most likely mean.

These details would of course have to be worked out by Congress, and would likely follow the patterns of success of the prior tax-deferral retirement savings plans, the IRAs and 401(k)s.

But personal investment accounts would presumably include these terms:

- ** Workers under some age (such as 21) would no longer have the option of having the 5.3% deducted as a payroll tax or of expecting Social Social retirement benefits. They would have to start with personal accounts or switch to making contributions to personal accounts.

- ** Workers over that age (such as 21 or older) would not be required to drop out of the Social Security retirement program, but would have that *option.* If they opt out, they would no longer have the 5.30% deducted as a payroll tax and would no longer expect to receive Social Security retirement benefits.

- ** Those workers who elect to stay in the Social Security retirement income plan could do so. They would be doing that with an understanding of the financial status of the plan, the understanding that payroll taxes might have to be increased in the future, and the understanding that the benefits might (as they have many times in the past) be increased or decreased.

- ** Those who opt out of the Social Security retirement income plan would then be given the advantage of having tax deferral on that part of their income (such as possibly 10%) that they would now put into a personal retirement account. And they would be required to set this money aside in such an account.

- ** The money in that account would be their own, in their own name, with regular statements, with stated beneficiaries, with the account's own tax-deferred earnings.

** Careful guidelines would be established for licensing of those banks, mutual funds or other financial institutions that the government would allow to manage these retirement accounts.

** Retirement would not be mandatory at some definite age, such as 65 or 70.

** Because the account holder would be the owner of these funds, at time of death any remaining funds would go to the chosen beneficiaries, such as the spouse or children.

** Some provision needs to be made for coverage of survivors, in order to provide something equivalent to what Social Security provided.

There are also several aspects of any privatization plan on which options have to be considered. For example, if people elect privatization should they also get guarantees that their retirement income will not be less than it might have been under Social Security? Those options will be reviewed later, when we get to the question of what our options are.

Therefore, privatization is basically a plan that gives almost all workers an *option*, a choice of whether they wish to stay with the present Social Security retirement income plan or to go on their own and provide for their own retirement incomes. No one over 21 (or some such age) is forced to choose privatization. But that option would become available.

It is worth noting that the nestegg that someone builds up by personal investing is not built up *only* until the time when that person retires. As money is drawn from the fund for use in the retirement years, the rest of the money can of course stay in the fund and go right on earning, right on through all the retirement years.

It may also be worth pointing out that those who elect to provide for their own retirement incomes get two tax advantages:

1. The 5.30% payroll tax is no longer taken out of the check. This is a tax cut of 5.3% of pay.

2. Whereas it had been necessary to also pay *income* tax on that 5.3% of payroll income, it would now *not* be necessary to pay income tax on that amount or on any additional amount of payroll that could now be put into a personal retirement savings account (such as up to 10.0% of payroll income).

So it would be a reduction in both payroll tax and income tax.

For those who want to read further about privatization, these are two of the best books and an excellent website:

"Promises to Keep – Saving Social Security's Dream," by Marshall N. Carter & William G. Shipman, 1996

"A New Deal for Social Security," by Peter J. Ferrara & Michael Tanner, 1998

www.socialsecurity.org (the website of The Cato Institute, with many links)

As is typical, we stop every once in a while to be sure that we are all still holding the pace and understanding what we

What Are the Facts about Investment and "Privatization"? 151

have covered, in this case about investment and privatization. We are ready to continue if you understand:

...the major difference between spending and investment, and what "return on investment" is.

...how invested money grows in value but money spent does not.

...the power of compound interest or compounded return on investment.

...the rule of 72, and how to figure how long it takes to double your money.

...how many years it would take you, for example, at 12% compounded, to grow $1,000 into $64,000.

...what average annual returns have been on large company stocks over the last 75 years.

...that the market goes up and down, particularly in short periods (such as daily, weekly, or even each year), but that over longer periods it has been very consistent and predictable.

...that short-term market performance shouldn't influence long-term decisions about privatization.

...the importance of regular saving, instead of trying to "time" purchases by figuring out special times to buy or sell.

...the kind of middle-of-the-road diversified large cap fund in which you want to invest, to minimize your risk.

...what an "expense ratio" is, and how low a percentage of the amount invested it can be.

...what the terms "defined benefit" and "defined contribution" mean.

...how "defined contribution" plans have taken over from "defined benefit" plans and why.

...how federal tax laws have been involved in these changes.

...how defined benefit and defined contribution plans are a responsibility issue.

...how there will be government restrictions on private retirement savings accounts, to further assure that they are as safe as possible.

...what "privatization" means, and who might choose that option.

...why privatization is being considered (at least two major reasons).

...what privatization has to accomplish with Social Security's future liabilities (its expected expenses)

...why "2%" plans won't get the job done.

...how, if there are costs (to the Social Security plan) of privatization, four things have to result from that cost (expense).

...the possibility that privatization may help present retirees and near-retirees be sure of getting their own benefits, which are presently in danger.

...that privatization is not mandatory, but is an option, a choice that some can make if they want to.

...that those who elect to stay in the Social Security retirement income plan have to do so with the understanding that payroll taxes may have to be increased in the future, that the plan faces financial difficulties and risks of its own, and that benefits are not guaranteed.

...what the basic provisions of a privatization plan would probably be.

...that privatization is in fact a double tax cut for those who make this selection.

Later on, we're going to look at the two related questions of, "Should I bail out of Social Security?" and "But how would we pay for those who stay with Social Security?"

Before getting to those questions, though, let's take a moment to see if we can learn anything about government retirement plans and privatization from other countries.

Question #9

What Can We Learn from Other Countries?

The United States is certainly not alone in having national pension system problems. Almost every developing or developed nation in the world, from the smallest to the largest, has problems about pensions. They either have to figure out what to do to start out right, or they are having to figure out how to get out of the impossible predicaments that their present systems have put them in. Few, if any, countries seem to have their pension problems solved.

But the international consensus is there, about what has shown itself to *not* work and about what *will* work.

If you have <u>physical</u> problems, the sensible thing is to see a doctor. Over many years of experience, the doctors have put together a body of knowledge about what good health is, what a person has to do to achieve it, and ways to measure whether a person is in good or poor health. In your physical examination, the doctor might determine, for example, that you are quite overweight, eating a high-fat diet, getting little exercise, and smoking a lot, with quite high cholesterol counts, high blood pressure and a heart that responded poorly to the treadmill test.

If you ask the doctor what all of that means, you will probably get at least two types of answers. First, the doctor will tell you that there has been an enormous amount of study done on all of these measurements, so we know what are good, bad, and very bad indicators (of results such as stroke, heart attacks, other disease and early death). The record is there to tell you what these indicators quite likely mean in your case.

But, secondly, the doctor will tell you that what you decide to do or not do with this information is your choice. It's up to you. The doctor can see your indicators of very bad health (which we might call "A"), knows that ideal health would be something we might call "Z," and that not everyone is going to have the courage or the will power to move all the way from "A" to "Z."

So, having been given this information by an expert, you might decide to do some comparison of your own, seeing what others are doing. And you find out that your friends are living lives that would probably result in health ratings for them all over the scale, from "A" to "Z."

The point is two-fold: although you may get good ideas from your friends as to *how* you can start making progress toward a healthier life, your goal is not to be *like* your friends but first to understand those *standards* that are already known to define good health. And secondly, even when you accept those standards as correct, a bigger question is going to be whether you are willing to do what needs to be done to go from bad to good health.

You have to define the standards that you know are correct, and then you have to decide whether you are going to do it right or settle for something less. We could say it gets down to two things: intelligence and willpower.

The same general ideas hold true when we start comparing fiscal (financial) health in the various countries' pension plans. There is a very extensive body of knowledge about pension plans in the world. One example would be "Social Security Programs Throughout the World," published by our Social

Security Administration. It is a 393-page encyclopedia of social programs covering nearly 150 nations, from Albania to Zimbabwe. You can get bogged down in the details very quickly, just as you could be wasting your time trying to study the physical health and life style of all your friends, as a guide to what you should be doing in your own life.

What we really need to do, in order to deal with this enormous amount of information that exists about pension plans in the world, is to extract from it the standards that tell us what works and what doesn't. Just as the physical doctor can tell us what the standards are for measuring good physical health, what can the fiscal doctors — those who have studied this history of pension plans — tell us works and doesn't work in the field of national pension plans?

Fortunately, they can tell us a lot. Some similar, major mistakes have been made by almost every developed nation, and the conclusions are inescapable. On the other hand, starting just over 20 years ago in Chile, and using all that has been learned from those prior mistakes, new standards and principles have been applied that appear to be quite successful in more and more countries.

It is one thing, though, to be thoroughly familiar with bad physical or fiscal health, and it is another thing to find that person or nation that will do *all* the right things so you can see a clean black-and-white record of what never works and what always works.

For one thing, the analysis of each county's pension or other social programs (such as workers' compensation or unemployment insurance) has to be set in the context of that county's degree of economic development. If the economy is based largely on barter, agriculture, self-employment, low levels of education, low GDP, no significant banking system, no stability in the government's control of inflation, etc., then we probably have little to learn from what this country is doing, because their circumstances are so different from ours.

Another question, when making county-to-country comparisons among more developed countries, is, "What is the status of their present pension programs?" How good or bad is the fiscal health of the country's pension plan to start with? Has the country had its present system for a long time, paying a high level of benefits, so that many people are counting on it and believe strongly in it, although it is clearly unsustainable? Or is the country able to start off essentially with a clean slate, moving toward the right kind of system without having the problem of first getting out of the present unworkable system? Usually, the problem is not to figure out what the ideal solution is. Instead, the problem is typically one of how to face up to or afford the transition out of the current mess.

As an example of one other difficulty of making comparisons, a country may have a totally bankrupt pension system, with runaway inflation and a very dissatisfied populace. But if the country is a dictatorship, then the dictator may be able to ram through immediate major change that would be entirely impossible in an established democracy. In the democracy, there has to be thorough leadership, communication and understanding that results in acceptance of the necessary decisions by the citizens themselves. Transitions in major democracies clearly call for much greater leadership.

Another way in which we can waste time looking for answers in comparisons would be, for example, in the many analyses that have been made of the cost of administering the mutual funds that were set up in Chile when that country established its then-revolutionary new pension plan. Chile was financially a relatively sophisticated market in 1980, guided by some advanced economists. But what that small country had to do back then in order to establish safe investment choices for its citizens, as they started investing major amounts of their savings, is simply not comparable to the situation in the United States today. If we want to know what an appropriate expense ratio is for managing invested funds in the US today, we have our *own* history of expense ratios on very large mutual funds and index funds, thrift plans and major pension plans. Regardless of what other countries did or are doing, we know from our own facts that these annual expenses can be less than 1% and probably less than 1/2 of 1% of the invested amounts. We have these answers for ourselves, without having to get them from others.

So, if we survey the history of pension plans of just the *major* countries of the *developed* world, what has worked and what hasn't worked for them? Let's start there, because the message is clear. Those countries got a slight head start on us, they are a bit further down the road ahead of us, and they are signaling back to us that it has turned out to be a dead end road. In fact, most of them can see the end of the road and are having a very hard time facing up to what to do next.

Historians trace the start of government-run national social retirement income assurance plans back to German Chancellor Otto von Bismarck, in 1889. In the next forty years, essentially every country in Europe adopted a similar program. Chile followed the Bismarck model in 1925, as all major countries of South America also adopted government-run plans. India, Russia, Japan and Canada followed suit during this time, too. The United States was among the last to introduce such a retirement income plan in 1935 legislation, although payments from the plan did not begin until 1940.

This was a period during which there was a major shift from agriculturally based economies to rapidly-increasing industry-based economies in these countries, with the resulting social instability and concern for its impact on the elderly.

These government-run retirement income plans of course had generally similar features. The income for them came from taxes paid by those working. The money was not "invested" in businesses or profit-making enterprises, but was simply used to pay the benefits that the government decided to pay retirees. They were, in our current terminology, pay-as-you-go defined benefit welfare programs for the elderly.

A common feature of such plans is that their financing is no problem as long as minimal benefits are promised, the economy is growing, and the number of retirees drawing benefits is low in ratio to the number of workers paying the taxes that finance those benefits. Also, to begin with, these taxes were a very low percent of payroll and the benefits were minimal or nonexistent. An example of this, that we have already covered, is that Social Security in the United States began paying when a person reached 65, and at that time the average life expectancy in the U.S. was less than 65.

So the introduction of government-paid retirement income began in the United States in 1940, more than 50 years after such programs began in Germany. And the general political philosophy in Europe was for more state responsibility for the welfare of the populace than was acceptable in the United States, where greater value was given to individual responsibility.

Someone might ask, "Why didn't at least some of these major countries start out with retirement income plans based on mandatory personal savings and investment?" The answer has to be that, at that early point in the progress of industrial societies and capitalism, it was obviously out of the question. The ownership of wealth was quite centralized and there were certainly no markets in which workers could be "investing" their saved money as they can today.

This is also to say that, although these state-run tax-based retirement assurance plans may have served their purpose in the early decades of the evolution of the industrial state, we now also know that these plans were destined to become the victims of predictable circumstances. The times have changed, the distribution of wealth has expanded, open capital markets exist for personal investment, and this growth of personal financial strength is translating into new opportunities for personal financial freedom and responsibility.

These Bismarck model state-run retirement assurance programs have deteriorated into major financial problems for basically five reasons.

The first is natural political overgenerosity. State-oriented politicians are prone to promise people more than they can deliver, and this is particularly possible with retirement income programs, where the cost of present promises may not come due for many years.

A second problem area has been inflation, which over these many years has totally devastated some economies and destroyed the value of money. A third problem has been corruption or government spending on other programs that meant that the government was simply left without enough money to pay its retirees what it had promised. In many cases, this problem came from the expectations of people that their governments could provide them with more than is possible for long.

For example, the 1999 issue of "Social Security Programs Throughout the World" shows these contribution rates for social security programs (in 1999) as percentages of payroll:

	Old-Age, Disability and Death	All Social Security Programs
Austria	22.80%	44.90%
Czech Republic	26.00%	47.50%
France	16.45%	49.89%
Germany	19.50%	41.20%
Hungary	30.00%	50.50%
Italy	32.70%	42.80%
Netherlands	37.72%	65.47%
Poland	35.52%	46.59%
Portugal	34.75%	37.75%
Spain	28.30%	38.08%
United States	12.40%	18.15%

(These percentages include amounts paid both by the insured person and the employer. "All Social Security Programs" includes Old-Age, Disability, Death; Sickness and Maternity; Work Injury; Unemployment; and Family Allowances. In some countries, the rate may not cover all of these programs. In some cases, only certain groups, such as wage earners, are represented. When the contribution rate varies, either the average rate or the lowest rate in the range is used.)

When (as is the case for the above-shown European countries), one third to two thirds of wage income is taxed and used by the government to provide social benefits, the role of the state becomes totally dominant over that of the individual. And the even stronger point is that (because of the two other problems that we have yet to cover), taxes as high as these are (as percentages of payroll) are *still* not enough to pay the ever-increasing costs of the promised benefits.

It is the fourth and fifth problems of state-run retirement income assurance programs that are the real clinchers, though:

longevity and fertility rates.

As these most advanced societies in the world develop, they improve their health and medical care, and so people live longer and longer. We've looked at the situation in the U.S., but it is typical of other developed countries too. So the retirees need retirement income for far more years than were originally expected.

For example, an outstanding 1994 study by the World Bank, "Averting the Old Age Crisis" (in Table A.2, starting on page 349 of the study), shows the Percentage of Population over Sixty Years Old, 1990-2150, from which we can extract these actual numbers for 1990 and projections for 2050:

	1990	2050
OECD Countries (Europe, Australia, New Zealand, Canada, UK and U.S.; Japan; basically the developed nations)	18.2%	31.2%
E. Europe & former Soviet Union	15.3%	26.5%
Latin America and Caribbean	6.9%	23.5%
Asia (including India and China)	7.4%	22.1%
Middle East and North Africa	7.0%	18.1%
Sub-Saharan Africa	4.6%	9.9%

The percentages were, of course, even lower back in the early 1900s, when the many state-run retirement income assurance programs were introduced.

But the other inevitable feature of developed societies is that the population starts to level off. The younger folks start having less children, and accordingly there are less workers per retiree. The cost of supporting more and more retirees falls on less and less workers. Sooner or later, that cost becomes too high. In Germany and Italy, for example, the forecast is that there will be one retiree for each worker within 30 years.

You have already seen the fertility rates in developed countries (such as 1.4 in Europe and 1.3 in Japan, when a rate of 2.1 generally means a stabilized population). These rates are extremely important for these nations. For example, in Europe this means there is a need for young immigrants from other countries to fill the need for workers. For politicians, it means having to face up to federal budgets with totally predictable impossible deficits.

Not understanding what was happening in these longer-term factors (political overpromising, government corruption or overspending, inflation, longer lives, and less children coming along), these countries are now belatedly realizing that they are truly on an economic dead-end road.

In a November 2000 commentary by David Fairlamb in the International Finance section of Business Week magazine, titled, "These Pension Plans Are No Panaceas," he dealt with European pension plans and summarized, "Instead, expect most governments to just tinker with their pension laws ... Fainthearted European policymakers know that such stopgap measures aren't enough, and they'll eventually have to allow privately managed, equity-based plans *a l'americaine.* Alas, they'll probably wait till catastrophe strikes before trying such a radical solution."

The facts are right there, for us to learn from, before we get any further into the same predicament that these earlier-starting pay-as-you-go defined benefit retirement income assurance programs have gotten into in all the major developed countries of the world.

The lessons are all around us, to teach us what *doesn't* work. What doesn't work any more is the pay-as-you-go defined-benefit government-run taxation-financed retirement income plan adopted 66 to 112 years ago by the major industrializing countries of the world, the last of those countries of course being the United States.

So what *does* work?

The recent rapid development of the "Asian Tiger" economies; the dissolution of the socialist Soviet Union; the economic revolution of the last 20 years in China; computers, the internet, television and increasingly open worldwide communication; the still-dominant performance of the economy of the United States; and the continuing surge in world trade and adoption of free enterprise principles all add up to tell the world that what works is *capitalism.*

Standards of living are increased through saving and investing in profit-producing businesses. Economies grow because of businesses, not because of governments. The proper role of government is now understood to be as the guardian of particular conditions: the rule of law, personal freedom, protection of personal property rights, "transparency" or openness about financial information for investors, proper monetary policy. Growth occurs where conditions attract financial investment and protect a return on that investment.

The world is learning that government-based socialism didn't produce as expected, and that personal freedom comes more as a result of increasing standards of living and the growth of personal economic power. Real personal freedom is based on real personal economic strength.

In essence, the best evolution of capitalism is expressed in the financial empowerment of the individual. In the American vision of freedom, the state or the government is there basically only to facilitate that personal freedom and responsibility.

So the plans that work best will be those that empower individuals. These plans will make individuals financially stronger and therefore more independent and free.

A century ago, there was a Bismarck model for establishment of a state-run pension income assurance plan. Today, there is a model for government support of savings plans by which individuals can use the power of compounded return on investment to provide for their own retirement incomes with far more flexibility and better results than government programs could ever have provided.

Certain conditions do have to exist for these new programs to work. But those conditions do exist, or can exist, in the developed countries of the world. The most developed country in the world is the United States, and it has the best conditions in which this new model can work.

This is not just theory, though, because in 1980 Mr. José Piñera, then Minister of Labor and Social Security in Chile, started the revolution in national pension plans. The previous plans in Chile, introduced there in 1925 on the Bismarck model, had reached the state of total failure in 50 years, and Mr. Piñera led the introduction of an entirely new system.

For that matter, he has gone on to become the world's leading "doctor" of national pension plans, as President of the International Center for Pension Reform. He consults with the major developed countries of the world, as they struggle to find ways to apply the lessons of Chile to their own countries. He has been the major force behind the privatization of the pension plans in most South American countries, is the major resource as to what is happening country-by-country in this world-wide pension plan revolution, and has testified before our Congress, spoken and written extensively on this subject in the U.S.

What he did in Chile had to be adapted to the circumstances (as is always the case), but adhered to sound universal economic principles. One reason that we find those free-enterprise principles so acceptable in our country is that he received both his master's degree and doctorate in economics in the U.S. at Harvard University.

The basic change made in Chile was that the money that

had previously been paid to the government as a tax now, instead, went into the worker's personal account, where it was that worker's property, invested to earn a compounded rate of return, so as to continue to belong to the worker, to provide for his or her retirement income needs, and with any balance going to the worker's heirs. The ownership and control of the property moved from the state to the individuals, empowering them with greater human dignity, freedom, and control over their own lives. Specifically, each worker automatically has 10 percent of his wages each month, during his working life, deposited by his employer in the employee's individual personal account. And the worker may contribute an additional 10 percent of wages each month, which is also deductible from taxable income, as a form of voluntary savings.

There were additional byproducts of this change in control and responsibility. Workers became shareholders, with the resulting change in the country's political dynamics. Ownership of stocks and bonds can change attitudes toward profits, the free enterprise system, and government. The greater amounts of saving and investment stimulate the growth of the economy. The essential link is re-established between effort and reward. People have new freedom to control their own retirement dates and futures. And, quite importantly, benefits of a plan based on private investment (instead of taxes) can be far greater.

As Mr. Piñera explained so clearly in testimony before U.S. Congressman Bill Archer's Ways and Means Committee hearing on February 3, 1999:

> "Now, the essence of the system is that we are allowing every worker, even the poorest worker in the country, to benefit from the extraordinary force of compounded interest. Every investor knows that if you keep money in an account for 40 years, the money gets interest over interest and, there-

fore, grows exponentially. And people who have high incomes have always had savings accounts and have, therefore, been able to benefit from that force. But, regrettably, the common worker, the simple worker, this person at the end of the month, after paying food, shelter, taxes, does not have additional income to save in an account. They have not been able to benefit from compounded interest. So, the essence of the Chilean system is to allow every worker, and especially the very poor, to benefit from the extraordinary force of compounded returns over their whole life."

He then went on to report on the results of the system:

"Well, the system has performed beyond all of our dreams because the average rate of return of the system during the last years ... has been 11 percent above inflation on the average every year."

And he spelled out three important rules that applied to the transition from their previous system to the new plan:

"The first one was that we guaranteed the benefits of the elderly people. So, every person who was already receiving a benefit in the Chilean system has nothing to fear from the reform. We gave a government guarantee that we would not take away our grandmother's check because those are promises made and those are promises that must be kept.

"The second important rule is that every young person who enters the work force goes into the system on the passbook account because we couldn't keep open the door of a system that we knew, because of demographic forces, would not be able to pay benefits in the future.

"And the third rule, and I would say that it is a very important rule, was that we gave every worker who was already in the labor force the option to stay in the government-run Social Security system, if they like it, or to move to the new system. So, it was a completely voluntary choice of every worker. So, by definition, nobody can be worse with a reform like this because, if someone doesn't like investing in the market, if someone doesn't like a passbook, if someone doesn't like compounded interest, they simply stay where they are."

And he later noted:

"Now, the extraordinary result has been that 95 percent of Chilean workers have chosen the new system even though there has been the usual discussion about market risk and so on, but people understand that, if you have a very conservative portfolio, you can reduce market risk to almost zero ... Those of you who have visited Chile, and I see a lot of faces here, have seen that the workers are happy with the new system. They are shareholders of the country. They are owners of the country's capital."

Also, in response to another Congressman's question, "How did you get the message out to individual Chileans that they had this opportunity, and convey to them, a potential for a return that exceeded the existing program?" Mr. Piñera noted:

"I believe that when you are doing a reform like this you have the duty to educate, to inform, to debate the system. So, we had a great effort of communication and education."

He then explained his extensive use of television spots, and concluded:

"So, I believe, sir, that it was not a gamble. I believe that you can trust it when you explain the ideas to them in simple, but truthful terms. And that is how it worked in Chile."

Later in his answering of questions, he made one other pertinent observation about the basic principles involved:

"The real force against this is those who do not want to lose the bureaucratic power because at the end of the day, this is a process of decentralizing power from the bureaucracy to the people."

Following Chile in 1980, and in many cases with Mr. Piñera's guidance, other countries have introduced private investment accounts, with provisions for workers to invest these percentages of their income in the accounts:

United Kingdom	1988 –1995	4.6%
Australia	1992	9% (as of 2002)
Peru	1993	10%
Argentina	1994	11%
Colombia	1994	10%
Uruguay	1995	varies
Bolivia	1997	10%
Mexico	1997	11.5%
Kazakhstan	1998	10%
El Salvador	1998	10%
Hungary	1998	6%
Poland	1999	9%

The United Kingdom's government pension system has been in continuing evolution, starting with Margaret Thatcher's 1986 introduction of an option for employees to open Personal Pension plans if they did not have Occupational (employer-offered) plans. The country's courage in facing its pension financing problems has resulted in the analysis by American Enterprise Institute scholar Carolyn Weaver that, "The United Kingdom is now in the enviable position of having no serious long-term Social Security debt problem. Yet many workers are gaining coverage under private pension arrangements that offer much higher returns than the government system. At the same time, a basic floor of protection remains."

Robert Moffitt of the Heritage Foundation also notes that the English system in 1999 had accumulated some $1.32 trillion in private assets and that, "This is slightly more than the size of the British economy, and larger than the private pension funds of all the other European countries combined."

The United Kingdom is an exception in Europe, in facing up to the need for change. As Peter Lilley, Member of Parliament in the United Kingdom, and former Secretary of State for Social Security reported to Congressman Bill Archer's House Ways and Means Committee in February 1999:

> "About 60 percent of people who are eligible to opt out of the state earnings-related pension do take advantage of that and ….that's 10 times what we anticipated when we introduced the scheme into personal pensions."

His prepared statement also contained an important note about "Public Acceptability":

> "In the UK the Labour Party has traditionally favoured state funded, pay-as-you-go pension provision. It was grudgingly

prepared to allow company schemes to opt out of the State Earnings Related Pension scheme. But it was critical both of the principle and the practice of allowing individuals to opt out of the state scheme into personal pensions.

"The emergence of the misselling problem and the Maxwell scandal gave them ammunition to fire at private funded pension provision. Despite that, the growing public popularity of private pension provision, coupled with increasing awareness of its long-term benefit to the public finances brought a gradual change of heart. Labour now plans to encourage more people to build up private funded pensions. Consequently, there is now more of a political consensus in Britain that private pension provision is a success; and that where possible more people should be enabled to opt out of the state system."

The testimony at that same hearing by David O. Harris, of Watson Wyatt Worldwide, brought out some interesting points about Australia's having moved its retirement system from reliance on pay-as-you-go and more toward a fully funded, defined contribution private investment:

"What is striking about the Australian system is that the political pressures are the reverse of those in the United States. There is a Federal Labor government, a largely liberal leaning administration, who has established and extended individual retirement accounts in 1987 and again in 1992. This policy is not only supported by organized labor but also is actively encouraged by the leadership of Australian Council of Trade Unions. Businesses and consumer groups also back the changes."

It would appear that the individual retirement account experience of labor in both the United Kingdom and Australia would be something that labor leaders in the United States would want to study and verify.

Possibly the "Concluding Thoughts" of the 1994 World Bank study, "Averting the Old Crisis," are the best summary:

"Around the world, countries are reevaluating their arrangements for providing income security for the old. As their populations age and their old age security systems consume an ever-increasing share of national resources, it becomes more and more important to get these arrangements right. Policymakers and citizens are finding that the old systems did not always deliver what they promised. Although each country has its own story, the problems of pension systems are surprisingly universal, rooted in demography and political economy. New options are available that promise to be better."

Yes, we can learn from the mistakes made in the past. And as the most free and financially advanced nation in the world, we have the conditions necessary for the introduction of retirement income plans that are appropriate for our times, and which therefore will give maximum responsibility to individuals for saving for, investing for, and planning their own retirements. Other countries, such as Chile, have shown us the way, and it is time for the United States to decide what is right and to lead the way.

This is no time for the world's most economically advanced nation to pussyfoot with 2% or 3% bandaids on an outdated pay-as-you-go system. It is time for the United States to boldly determine how to finance the transition to full privatization of its retirement income system.

Question #10

Should I Bail Out of Social Security?

After someone understands the basic facts of the federal budget, Social Security, and investment, the next question can be, "Then if I pull out of Social Security and instead invest that money, will I be able to do as well as I would have under Social Security?"

There are quite a few things that would really need to be considered before making that decision, but one major factor would be some actual calculations of (1) what it appears that Social Security might be paying you when you retire, and (2) what you might make by instead investing money in a personal retirement account.

This chapter is the one with the heaviest number work, so hang in there for this chapter and you will have made it through the tough part.

If you are looking 20 to 40 years into the future, the numbers are going to be higher because of inflation. So remember that we are not looking at "constant" dollars (which means assuming that there would no inflation) but at "current" dollars (meaning that there would be inflation).

That then introduces the question, "But what *rate* of inflation?" To keep any comparisons (of Social Security to personal accounts) fair, we are going to use the same inflation rate in either case. And to keep it simpler, we are going to use only

Social Security's "intermediate" or middle-of-the-road estimate, which is that inflation will average 3.3%, wages will go up that much plus 1.0% more each year, so wages will go up 4.3% each year (compared to the prior year).

That means that, on the personal savings side of our comparison, we will also be assuming that your salary or wages go up an average of 4.3% per year. So those are the main assumptions about (1) inflation and (2) wage increases over the years between now and when you retire.

With those qualifications in mind, let's do the Social Security calculations first.

What Social Security might provide

To make the calculations about expected Social Security benefits, we also have to start with the assumption that the Social Security plan will stay the same, providing the same benefits, and being *able* to pay those benefits when you retire.

But using those assumptions, the annual reports of the Social Security trustees *do* give information as to what benefits Social Security expects to be paying in certain years in the future. On page 177 you will find Table 10-1, "Estimated Annual Benefits Payable to Retired Workers," from the trustees' year 2000 report.

On that Table 10-1, there are 4 columns under the heading "Retirement at normal retirement age," and the left-hand column shows how the normal retirement age is already scheduled to increase from 65 to 67. That schedule of increased retirement dates may well be changed soon, so the "normal retirement age" on which benefits starts becomes 68, 69, or 70. To keep our comparison simple, and in even 5-year periods, we are going to skip these 4 columns on the left and use only the 3 columns on the right, where the heading is "Retirement at age 65."

TABLE 10-1: Estimated Annual Benefit Amount Payable to Retired Workers with Various Steady Pre-Retirement Earnings Levels Based on Intermediate Assumptions, Calendar Years 2000-2075

Year attain age 65 [2]	Age at retirement	Retirement at normal retirement age Current dollars	Constant 2000 dollars [3]	Percent of Earnings	Retirement at age 65 Current dollars	Constant 2000 dollars [3]	Percent of earnings
LOW EARNINGS: [4]							
2000	65:0	$ 7,194	$7,194	52.8	$ 7,194	$ 7,194	52.8
2005	65:6	9,674	8,172	56.5	9,205	7,903	54.9
2010	66:0	12,178	8,606	56.6	10,962	8,002	53.2
2015	66:0	14,993	9,007	56.5	13,501	8,379	53.1
2020	66:2	18,606	9,452	56.4	16,461	8,685	52.4
2025	67:0	23,693	9,959	56.2	19,096	8,565	49.3
2030	67:0	29,252	10,453	56.2	23,573	8,989	49.3
2035	67:0	36,099	10,967	56.2	29,096	9,433	49.3
2040	67:0	44,570	11,512	56.2	35,918	9,900	49.3
2045	67:0	55,015	12,080	56.2	44,330	10,387	49.3
2050	67:0	67,903	12,676	56.2	54,726	10,902	49.3
2055	67:0	83,822	13,303	56.2	67,553	11,440	49.3
2060	67:0	103,460	13,959	56.2	83,376	12,004	49.3
2065	67:0	127,718	14,650	56.2	102,918	12,598	49.3
2070	67:0	157,632	15,372	56.2	127,032	13,219	49.3
2075	67:0	194,573	16,131	56.2	156,801	13,872	49.3
AVERAGE EARNINGS:							
2000	65:0	11,875	11,875	39.2	11,875	11,875	39.2
2005	65:6	15,992	13,509	42.0	15,209	13,058	40.8
2010	66:0	20,143	14,234	42.2	18,109	13,219	39.5
2015	66:0	24,787	14,891	42.0	22,285	13,830	39.4
2020	66:2	30,756	15,624	41.9	27,182	14,341	38.9
2025	67:0	39,227	16,489	41.9	31,526	14,141	36.6
2030	67:0	48,421	17,304	41.9	38,915	14,840	36.6
2035	67:0	59,768	18,158	41.9	48,036	15,573	36.6
2040	67:0	73,775	19,055	41.9	59,298	16,343	36.6
2045	67:0	91,066	19,997	41.9	73,185	17,148	36.6
2050	67:0	112,412	20,985	41.9	90,343	17,997	36.6
2055	67:0	138,740	22,019	41.9	111,509	18,885	36.6
2060	67:0	171,242	23,105	41.9	137,633	19,816	36.6
2065	67:0	211,384	24,247	41.9	169,893	20,796	36.6
2070	67:0	260,911	25,444	41.9	209,687	21,821	36.6
2075	67:0	322,040	26,699	41.9	258,830	22,898	36.6
HIGH EARNINGS: [5]							
2000	65:0	15,387	15,387	31.7	15,387	15,387	31.7
2005	65:6	20,996	17,737	34.5	19,963	17,140	33.5
2010	66:0	26,557	18,767	34.7	23,934	17,471	32.7
2015	66:0	32,682	19,634	34.6	29,445	18,274	32.5
2020	66:2	40,566	20,607	34.6	35,919	18,951	32.2
2025	67:0	51,609	21,694	34.4	41,659	18,686	30.2
2030	67:0	63,702	22,765	34.4	51,429	19,612	30.2
2035	67:0	78,623	23,887	34.4	63,474	20,578	30.2
2040	67:0	97,046	25,066	34.4	78,347	21,594	30.2
2045	67:0	119,788	26,304	34.4	96,709	22,660	30.2
2050	67:0	147,861	27,603	34.4	119,368	23,779	30.2
2055	67:0	182,504	28,965	34.4	147,344	24,953	30.2
2060	67:0	225,258	30,393	34.4	181,867	26,185	30.2
2065	67:0	278,047	31,894	34.4	224,487	27,478	30.2
2070	67:0	343,193	33,468	34.4	277,072	28,833	30.2
2075	67:0	423,610	35,120	34.4	342,002	30,257	30.2
MAXIMUM EARNINGS: [6]							
2000	65:0	17,241	17,241	23.7	17,241	17,241	23.7
2005	65:6	24,119	20,375	26.0	22,935	19,692	25.2
2010	66:0	31,454	22,227	27.1	28,181	20,572	25.3
2015	66:0	39,420	23,683	27.5	35,413	21,977	25.8
2020	66:2	49,134	24,960	27.6	43,452	22,926	25.6
2025	67:0	62,668	26,342	27.5	50,502	22,653	24.2
2030	67:0	77,384	27,654	27.5	62,367	23,783	24.1
2035	67:0	95,494	29,012	27.5	76,976	24,955	24.1
2040	67:0	117,719	30,405	27.5	94,893	26,154	24.1
2045	67:0	145,310	31,908	27.5	117,130	27,445	24.1
2050	67:0	179,316	33,475	27.5	144,552	28,795	24.1
2055	67:0	221,311	35,124	27.5	178,402	30,213	24.1
2060	67:0	273,161	36,857	27.5	220,204	31,705	24.1
2065	67:0	337,176	38,677	27.5	271,801	33,270	24.1
2070	67:0	416,173	40,585	27.5	335,480	34,911	24.1
2075	67:0	513,677	42,587	27.5	414,091	36,634	24.1

Source: Pages 185-6, The 2000 Annual Report of the Board of Trustees of the Federal Old-Age and Survivors Insurance and Disability Insurance Trust Funds, U.S. Government Printing Office

And out of those 3 columns on the right, we are going to use only two: "current dollars" (meaning that those dollars allow for inflation) and "Percent of earnings."

Now we can use those two columns to figure out how much someone's "steady pre-retirement earnings levels" (on which the benefits are calculated) would be. It's simple. Take the top line, for example. The current dollars of benefits (for those with low earnings) were $7,194 in the year 2000. That was 52.8% of earnings. So you divide $7,194 by 52.8%, and find that the earnings would be $13,625. (Check: $13,625 x 52.8% = $7,194).

Then we can pull numbers out of those two columns to make up the table below, for people who were (on January 1, 2000, to keep it simple and in 5-year periods), 25, 30, 35, 40, 45 (and as a comparison to now) 65 years old.

Age, 1/1/2000	25	30	35	40	45	65
Born, 1/1 of yr:	1975	1970	1965	1960	1955	1935
Retiring at 65, in the year:	2040	2035	2030	2025	2020	2000
Years to retirement:	40	35	30	25	20	0
Low earnings:	$72,856	$59,018	$47,815	$38,734	$31,414	$13,625
X % of earnings:	x 49.3%	x 49.3%	x 49.3%	x 49.3%	x 52.4%	x 52.8%
= Benefits:	$35,918	$29,096	$23,573	$19,096	$16,461	$ 7,194
Ave. earnings:	$162,016	$131,246	$106,325	$ 86,137	$69,877	$30,293
X % of earnings:	x 36.6%	x 36.6%	x 36.6%	x 36.6%	x 38.9%	x 39.2%
= Benefits:	$ 59,298	$ 48,036	$ 38,915	$ 31,526	$ 27,182	$11,875
High earnings:	$259,427	$210,179	$170,295	$137,944	$111,550	$48,539
X % of earnings:	x 30.2%	x 30.2%	x 30.2%	x 30.2%	x 32.2%	x 31.7%
= Benefits:	$ 78,347	$ 63,474	$ 51,429	$ 41,659	$ 35,919	$15,387

We need to "walk through" this above information to make sure it's clear. For example, if on January 1, 2000 you were 25 years old, you had 40 more years of work until you would retire at age 65 in the year 2040. If you had a *low* pre-retirement earnings level (around $73,000 per year at the time you retired –that being equivalent to $13,625 now), your annual Social Security benefit would be $35,918.

Or, as another example, if on January 1, 2000 you were 35 years old, you had 30 more years to work until you would retire at age 65 in the year 2030. If you had an *average* pre-retirement earnings level (around $106,000 per year at the time you retired – that being equivalent to $30,293 now), your annual Social Security benefit would be $38,915.

Or, for one more example, if on January 1, 2000 you were 45 years old, you had 20 more years to work until you would retire at age 65 in the year 2020. If you had a *high* average pre-retirement earnings level (around $111,500 per year at the time you retired – that being equivalent to $48,539 now), your annual Social Security benefit would be $35,919.

On the above table you can also again see how the payout formula is slanted toward those with low income, so they get a payout that is a higher percentage of their final income. (For example, 49.3% of earnings for those with low earnings, 36.6% of earnings for those with average earnings, and 30.2% of earnings for those with high earnings. And as the earnings go even higher, the percentage keeps getting lower.)

That is important when people start calculating whether they can do better "on their own." It is going to be easier to save in order to retire with 30.2% of your income than it would be to retire with 49.3% of your income.

That also means that those with lower income are going to be the real test of whether privatization can provide at least equal retirement income. That is so because the present Social

Security system expects to provide the lower income workers with a retirement income that is a higher percentage of their final working pay.

We'll evaluate all of this in more detail later, but for now the above should give you some idea of what numbers you would try to equal or exceed if you went "on your own," leaving Social Security and instead investing your own money in your own account.

We now have some "benchmarks" of what Social Security might provide, and that puts us in a position to see what personal investment returns it would take, over how many years, to equal or better those government benefits.

What personal investment might provide

There are all sorts of possibilities to consider, but we're going to pick a few as examples. You can then do your own calculations later, using other numbers.

First, we're using the ages shown above (25, 30, 35, 40 and 45), and the related numbers of years left for people of these ages (40, 35, 30, 25, and 20) until they reach normal retirement ages of 65.

Secondly, the assumption in these following examples is that (1) the 5.3% of the person's income that had been deducted from taxable income to go to Social Security for retirement will no longer be deducted, and the employee will accordingly agree to no longer expect to receive retirement benefits from Social Security, (2) the remaining 2.35% of pay that had been deducted from taxable income to cover Disability Insurance and Medicare will still be deducted, with no change, (3) the total of 7.65% that the *employer* pays for Social Security retirement and disability and for Medicare will still be paid, with no change, but (4) the employee will now invest 10.0% of taxable income in a special retirement account, with this 10.0% of income no longer now being considered as taxable. In other words, this 10.0% will be treated in the same way that deposits to IRAs are now treated (although IRAs would be separate accounts).

Thirdly, there are two assumptions about the rate at which these invested funds will grow and compound over the years. To stay consistent with the Social Security assumptions, we start with an expectation that wages will go up 4.3% per year (that being as a result of a combination of cost-of-living and merit increases each year). Then, on top of that, the two assumptions are that (1) the invested money will make a 10%/year return (which is less than the market average return over the last 75 years), or (2) an 8%/year return, that being a return that is *more than twenty five percent below* the historical market return.

With those assumptions, we can put together a set of numbers and then review what they mean:

First, we start with the same year 2000 earnings that were used in the Social Security examples: "Low" was $13,625/year, "average" was $30,293/year, and "high" was $48,539/year. Those three numbers translate into investments of $113.54/month, $252.44/month, and $404.49/month in the year 2000, (those numbers being 10% of monthly salary or wages in every case). People at these three different income levels start putting these amounts aside every month in the year 2000 in personal retirement savings accounts.

Secondly, these amounts increase two ways: (a) they earn at a compounded rate of either 8.0% or 10.0%, and (b) there are annual wage increases of 4.3%.

Thirdly, you know that these people have 20, 25, 30, 35, or 40 years in which to save and compound the return on these savings.

You now have the three pieces of information that you need

(amount you are putting in, interest rates at which the money will earn, and years), in order to develop the following table:

Nest eggs that can be developed in personal retirement accounts

Age in Yr 2000:	25	30	35	40	45
Years to Invest:	40	35	30	25	20

Low Income
($13,625/yr = $1135.42/month x 10% = $113.54/mo in year 2000):

| @ 8.0% | $ 625,000 | $ 399,000 | $ 250,000 | $ 152,000 | $ 90,000 |
| @ 10.0% | $1,000,000 | $ 595,000 | $ 349,000 | $ 200,000 | $ 110,000 |

Average Income
($30,293/yr = $2,524.42/mo x 10% = $252.44/mo in year 2000):

| @ 8.0% | $1,390,000 | $ 887,000 | $ 555,000 | $ 339,000 | $ 199,000 |
| @ 10.0% | $2,222,000 | $1,323,000 | $ 776,000 | $ 444,000 | $ 246,000 |

High Income
($48,539/yr = $4,044.92/mo x 10% = $404.49/mo in year 2000):

| @ 8.0% | $2,227,000 | $1,421,000 | $ 890,000 | $ 543,000 | $ 319,000 |
| @ 10.0% | $3,561,000 | $2,120,000 | $1,243,000 | $ 712,000 | $ 394,000 |

To review what that table means: for example, someone age 25 with *low* income (starting around $13,600 per year in the year 2000) saves for 40 years until retirement at age 65 and would accumulate either $625,000 (at 8.0%) or $1,000,000 (at 10.0%).

Another example: someone age 35, with *average* income (starting around $30,000 per year in the year 2000) saves for 30 years until retirement at age 65 and would accumulate either

$555,000 (at 8.0%) or $776,000 (at 10.0%).

And someone age 45, with *high* income (starting around $48,500 per year in the year 2000) saves for 20 years until retirement at age 65 and would accumulate either $319,000 (at 8.0%) or $394,000 (at 10.0%).

So you can see from the above that after a certain number of years the compounding really takes hold and starts increasing the totals. But it does therefore take a certain number of years to build up this nest egg.

Comparing Social Security to a personal retirement savings account

Now comes the question of how you compare (1) an amount that a retiree would start getting monthly from Social Security in the first year of retirement, with that amount then going up each year by an inflation adjustment with (2) a lump sum accumulated in an account by that same first year of retirement.

In other words, how can you compare a monthly *income* (that will be increased to keep up with inflation in later years) with *a lump sum*?

There are basically two ways to do it:

1. By finding out what monthly income you would get from your accumulated nest egg if you bought an "annuity" with it, and

2. By calculating what monthly income you could take out of your nest egg (while you kept the balance invested and earning) without running out of money in your lifetime.

Annuities

In order to analyze the possibility of taking out an "annuity," we need to be sure you at least understand a few basics about what an annuity is.

Basically, it is an arrangement whereby you would give a certain amount of money (say $100,000) to a financial concern in exchange for their agreeing to give you a steady monthly payment. You could have the payments run for a set period of years (such as 10 or 20) or for life. If the annuity is for "life," now it is a gamble. You and the insurance company are betting on your life expectancy. They will pay you based on the averages. If you live less years than the average, the insurance company comes out ahead. If you live more years than the average, you come out ahead.

But with a "life annuity" you give up your lump sum of money and pay someone else to invest that money, take the risk, (make some money for taking that risk), and to be sure you get your income at a steady rate for the rest of your life, however long that may be.

One problem with a regular life annuity, however, is that it is typically an unchanging monthly amount. The problem is of course inflation, which makes those dollars worth less and less each year. With even 3% inflation, money is worth half as much in 24 years.

So the insurance companies also offer "inflation-indexed life annuities," an example being an annuity that starts at one monthly amount the first year, but then goes up 3% the next year and 3% every year after that. However, if the amount is going to keep getting larger every year, it is going to start out being less in the first year. In general, for a person at age 65 the inflation-indexed life annuity might start out paying 75 – 80% as much as the straight annuity. For a person at age 70, it might start out paying around 80% as much.

To compare fairly with Social Security (which is in effect an inflation-indexed life annuity), you need to figure out how much of an inflation-indexed life annuity you could buy with your nest egg. Then you can see if that would be more or less than what you would be getting from Social Security.

So let's do that. This has to be done with the qualification, though, that annuity rates change over time, with changes in interest rates. But we will have to work with the rates that are available at present. A positive aspect of this might also be that, if there were to be a major increase in the use of annuities, as a result of privatization, there would undoubtedly be even more competition and better rates.

To simplify this subject as much as possible, our rules of thumb are going to be that:

1. If you get the inflation-indexed life annuity at age <u>65</u>, it will start out paying you an annual total (in monthly payments) equal to about <u>one fourteenth</u> (1/14) of the amount you paid for it (your nest egg).
2. If you get the inflation-indexed life annuity at age <u>70</u>, it will start out paying you an annual total (in monthly payments) equal to about <u>one-twelfth</u> (1/12) of the amount you paid for it (your nest egg).

Since we have been comparing Social Security with personal retirement savings accounts as of age <u>65</u>, we will use the 1/14 rule of thumb. What this rule says is that if you paid $100,000 for this inflation-indexed annuity, it would start off paying you 1/14 of that amount – or $7,143 — the first year.

So what we do is simply divide any nest egg amount by 14 and see if it is more or less than what we might be getting from Social Security.

Rather than make you do a lot of dividing by 14, though, we'll do it for you and try to put it all together in one table that makes the comparison:

SAVING SOCIAL SECURITY (FROM CONGRESS)

1/14 of the nest egg would provide a life annuity per year, starting at this amount in the year of retirement, and going up 3% every year

If your age is:
— 25 — — 30 — — 35 — — 40 — — 45 —

And you retire at age 65 with LOW earnings:
Social Security pays (per year):
$ 35,918 $29,096 $23,573 $19,096 $16,461
And 1/14 of your accumulated personal retirement account would be:
@ 8.0% $ 44,658 $28,485 | $17,840 $10,889 $ 6,396
@10.0% $ 71,400 $42,508 $24,915 | $14,272 $ 7,891

Or you retire at age 65 with AVERAGE earnings:
Social Security pays (per year):
$ 59,298 $48,036 $38,915 $31,526 $27,182
And 1/14 of your accumulated personal retirement account would be:
@ 8.0% $ 99,289 $63,332 $39,665 | $24,210 $14,221
@10.0% $158,746 $94,510 $55,394 $31,731 | $17,544

Or you retire at age 65 with HIGH earnings:
Social Security pays (per year):
$ 78,347 $63,474 $51,429 $41,659 $35,919
And 1/14 of your accumulated personal retirement account would be:
@ 8.0% $159,093 $101,477 $63,556 | $38,792 $22,786
@10.0% $254,362 $151,434 $88,759 $50,843 | $22,111

Some review of those above numbers:

1. With *low* earnings, all the 25, 30 and 35-year-olds would be better off with the personal retirement accounts, with the exception of the 35-year-old with only an 8.0% return. The 35-year-old with the 8.0% return, and all the 40 and 45-year-olds would be better off with Social Security in all these low earnings examples.

2. With *average* earnings, all the 25, 30 and 35-year-olds would be better off with the personal retirement account. The 40-year-old with a 10.0% return would have a close decision. The 40-year-old with only an 8.0% return and all the 45-year-olds would be better off with Social Security.

3. With *high* earnings, all the 25, 30 and 35-year-olds would definitely be better off with the personal retirement account. The 40-year-old with a 10.0% return would also be better off with the personal retirement account. The 40-year-old with the 8.0% return and all the 45-year-olds would be better off with Social Security.

4. In summary, all the 25, 30 and 35-year-olds would be better off with personal retirement accounts (except the 35-year-old with low earnings and only an 8.0% compounding), because they had 30 to 40 years in which their savings could compound in value. For many of them, the personal retirement account would produce a return that is *many* times that of Social Security's. For those who are *younger* than 25 (not shown on the table), with more than 40 years in which to compound their earnings, the difference between the personal account and Social Security would be even more in favor of the personal account.

5. Among the 40-year-olds, those with *low* earnings would be

better off staying with Social Security, because 20 to 25 years was not a long enough time in which to compound the value of the personal savings account. However, the 40-year-olds with *average* or *high* income (which Social Security defines as the equivalent of earnings of about $30,300 or $48,500 in the year 2000) could do better with the personal retirement accounts either if they earned the 10.0% return or if they had earnings even higher than what Social Security calls "high" in these examples. All the 45-year-olds with 8% returns over their 25-year investment terms were better off staying with Social Security. And all 45-year-olds were better off staying with Social Security, unless they had even higher incomes than shown here.

6. If these above numbers were all that people considered, then almost all workers 35 and under would elect personal retirement accounts, the workers around the age of 40 would need average or higher income and 10% returns in order to elect the personal retirement accounts, and all workers 45 or older would stay with Social Security (unless they had income even higher than shown here, and 10% or better returns).

In analyzing these numbers, though, the first thing to remember is that they are certainly not as exact as they might appear. One number may be "$35,918" (from Social Security) or "$44,658" (from personal investment) above, but what might actually happen in 40 years could be off by thousands of dollars.

Later on, we'll deal with some other reservations about the above comparison (of Social Security to an annuity purchased by your nest egg). But the above is at least a way by which to compare the two.

Drawing a monthly pension from your own nest egg

There were two ways mentioned to compare the Social Security income to the nest egg. The first was to change the nest egg into an inflation-indexed life annuity. The second method might be for you to simply keep the money invested yourself and to draw a regular monthly pension out of it, while the remaining amount continues to earn.

If you retire, you stop earning and having your wages go up. So thereafter the returns are simply 8.0% or 10.0% (to continue our examples).

We'll go through the calculations, if you want to study them, but they will show essentially the same thing that the annuity analysis did. If the annuity analysis showed that someone would be better off with Social Security or with the personal retirement account, this following analysis will generally show the same thing (although now also showing the personal retirement account as more favorable for high income 40 and 45-year-olds).

It's too complicated to calculate how long the nest egg would last if (1) payments are being taken out at a rate that is increasing, with inflation, every year, and (2) the amount that would remain is earning 8% or 10%. So, to keep it a little simpler, we are going to calculate how long the nest egg would last if (1) *the same amount* is taken out every year, and (2) the amount that would remain is earning 8% or 10%.

Taking an equal amount out each month is like a *regular* annuity, but it is *not* comparable to the *inflation-adjusted life annuity* that Social Security would provide. To *be* comparable with Social Security, the straight annuity number is going to need to be 25% to 35% more than what Social Security starts out paying.

In the years that we are talking about (2020–2040), Social Security expectations are that men who reach 65 will live about another 18 to 20 years, and the women will live about another 21 to 23 years. To be a little conservative, we will do the calculations on the assumption that, at age 65, you want the nest egg to last 25 years more, until you would be 90.

The way the calculations can be done is on any computer program that tells you how much the annual payment is for a 25-year loan of some amount, if you are charged either 8% or 10% interest. One such program is Microsoft Money/ Planning Wizards/ Loan Calculator.

For example, you enter these facts: Loan amount: $625,000 (which is the nest egg a 25-year-old with low earnings would have after 40 years of investment). Interest rate: 8% (what the money will keep earning). Loan Length: 25 years. Payment frequency: annual (to keep comparisons simple). Payment amount: (leave this blank, because this is what you are trying to find out). Balloon amount: zero. Click on "Calculate." It will fill in the "payment amount" as $58,569.

That means that this low earnings person with $625,000 invested at 8.0% at retirement could get payments of $58,569 each year out of that account for the next 25 years. (That totals up to $1,464,000) The $58,569 is clearly more than 25% or 35% in excess of the $35,918 that Social Security projects that it would provide under the same circumstances.

If we go ahead and fill out the table on the basis of the nest egg amounts that we figured out earlier, this table tells you how much you could take out as an unchanging amount each year for the 25 years after you retire at 65, if you have the balance earning either 8% or 10%. At the end of the 25 years, the money would be gone.

Should I Bail Out of Social Security?

Even annual payments that could be taken out of the nest egg for 25 years

(These payments could come monthly, but are shown here annually, to make the comparisons simpler):

If your age is:
— 25 —   — 30 —   — 35 —   — 40 —   — 45 —

And you retire at age 65 with LOW earnings:
Social Security pays (per year):
    $ 35,918 $ 29,096 $ 23,573 $19,096 $16,461
And your annual payment from your nest egg for 25 years would be:
@ 8% $ 58,569 $ 37,358 $ 23,397 $14,281 $ 8,388
@10% $110,124 $ 65,562 $ 38,428 $22,012 $12,170

Or you retire at age 65 with AVERAGE earnings:
Social Security pays (per year):
    $ 59,298 $ 48,036 $ 38,915 $31,526 $27,182
And your annual payment from your nest egg for 25 years would be:
@ 8% $130,218 $ 83,060 $ 52,021 $31,752 $18,651
@10% $244,843 $145,767 $ 85,438 $48,940 $27,059

Or you retire at age 65 with HIGH earnings:
Social Security pays (per year):
    $ 78,347 $ 63,474 $ 51,429 $41,659 $35,919
And your annual payment from the nest egg for 25 years would be:
@ 8% $208,651 $133,088 $ 83,354 $50,876 $29,884
@10% $392,315 $233,565 $136,898 $78,418 $43,357

Again, the way of comparing is that the annual payment from the nest egg would have to be 25% to 35% better than what Social Security pays in order for the personal retirement account option to be better. Another way to say it is that if the *regular* unchanging amount checks out as 25% to 35% better than Social Security, then that tells you that you could, if you wanted to, start taking money out at the lower rate and then increase it every year with inflation and still be ahead of Social Security.

A summary of the two numerical comparisons

In broad summary, both of these ways of comparing that lump sum to Social Security come up with the same conclusions: (1) almost all workers 35 and under would do better electing personal retirement accounts, (2) workers 40 years old with *average* incomes and 10% returns, or *high* incomes, would do better with personal retirement accounts, whereas those with *low* incomes or returns would do best to stay with Social Security, and (3) almost all 45-year-olds would do better to stay with Social Security, except for those with "high" incomes — as defined here by Social Security, equivalent to about $48,500 in the year 2000 — or higher.

And that brings us to the things that have to be considered or compared, in *addition* to the above kind of arithmetic.

Comparisons other than the numbers

The trouble with all of the above number work is of course that it is all based on a bunch of assumptions about how things will be 20 to 40 years from now. The conclusions are only as good as the assumptions on which they are based.

So let's review the assumptions, to see which ones you have

more or less faith in. For example:

Will you have low, average, or high earnings in the years between now and when you retire? Will you get average, or lower or higher than average, wage or salary increases over those years?

How sound is the Social Security retirement system, when it will begin running a cash deficit by around the year 2015 (and maybe earlier) and the trustees openly say that the plan will be paying only 72% of benefits by the year 2039, *even if* Congress (1) pays back the trillion or so dollars that it has taken from the trust fund, (2) pays interest for what it has borrowed, and (3) is kept from having any access to the trust fund after that. If the funds won't be there to pay the benefits, then that changes the entire comparison of Social Security versus private investment.

On the other hand, is it realistic to expect that 8%, or 10% can be earned on average on money invested conservatively over the next 20 to 40 years, even if that is below the historical record for the last 75 years? Is it likely that the return might be less, or maybe even more? Are the economic trends in the United States and the world such that we should expect continuation of the same trends, less, or more?

The numbers may come up with "answers." But those answers are only as good as your belief in the assumptions on which those answers are built. You have to weigh the odds of the Social Security numbers coming true versus the odds of the personal investment results coming true.

There is no way to avoid risk. There is risk either way.

Question #11

But How Will We Pay for Those Who Stay with Social Security?

One of the obvious concerns of those who see the younger generations considering "bailing out" of Social Security is, "But who is going to pay for *my* Social Security retirement benefits, if we don't have all of this payroll tax revenue coming in from the kids?"

Good question. If Social Security has a forecast of enormous future deficits, with outgo far exceeding income, how can anyone support a plan that would decrease Social Security's income even *more*?

This is, of course, also a fear that some politicians have been able to capitalize on, to their own advantages, but in fact probably not to the advantage of the seniors.

Achieving balance

The general answer is that there have to be tradeoffs. There are disadvantages of having people leave Social Security, but there are also more than offsetting advantages.

In the near term, these younger people who leave Social Security would no longer be paying their payroll taxes as income into Social Security. But the main point is that in the longer term, they would no longer be adding to the future liabilities of

Social Security, the future obligations to pay out amounts that have been promised with no known way of fulfilling those promises.

And those ever-escalating future obligations are at present the unsolvable problem.

The paradox is that, if the transition is done correctly, the loss of income in the near term will eliminate the liabilities (the obligations in the future) so that the actual net result is the protection of the benefits of those who *do* stay in the Social Security retirement program.

The real problem is to balance the needs of *everyone*, so it can be to the advantage of many to leave the program but also be to the advantage of others to stay with the program. It is no solution if one group takes care of itself, to the disadvantage of the others.

We also need to again remind ourselves that it is no honest or fair solution if all groups take care of themselves to the disadvantage of our children and grandchildren.

A transition proposal

There are three major ingredients that have to be dealt with in any solution. Those are (1) the escalating deficit itself, (2) the limited years that we have left until the number of retirees suddenly will be increasing so much, and (3) the present one-time buildup of money predicted in the Social Security retirement trust fund.

First, let's review those three ingredients. After that, we'll review ways in which those three ingredients can be mixed together to reach a solution.

The escalating deficit problem, in chart form

The first ingredient of any solution is the deficit problem itself. On Chart 11-1, page 198, you can see the deficit problem (shown this time for only the OASI, or retirement, fund). Skip the two lines that start in the middle and curve down to the right.

Look first at the two lines that start in the lower left and curve upward to the right. The first one that we want to look at is the top one of those two lines, which shows the expected "outgos" (the money that has to be paid out as checks to retirees) in the years from now through 2039. The chart doesn't go on out to 2075 because the trust fund runs out of money in 2039. As you can see on the chart, the prediction is that the cash outgos of this fund will be more than a trillion dollars per year in excess of the cash income of the fund in the year 2039. And as you can also see, the gap between cash outgos and cash income keeps getting larger and larger.

This increasing outgo line is a necessary first part of any solution. We have to do something about it.

The limited time left until the number of retirees surges

You will recall, from reviewing the information in the section, "Are we ready to talk?" that starting somewhere between the years 2010 and 2015, the number of retirees will be increasing faster than the number of workers. Then over the 20 years from 2010 to 2030 we will be adding about 2.4 retirees for every worker that we add.

If we are going to do anything about paying for this expected surge of retirees, who will stop being workers and start being recipients of checks in 10 or 15 years, we need to do it in the next 10 to (at the most) 15 years. After that, the problem will

198   SAVING SOCIAL SECURITY (FROM CONGRESS)

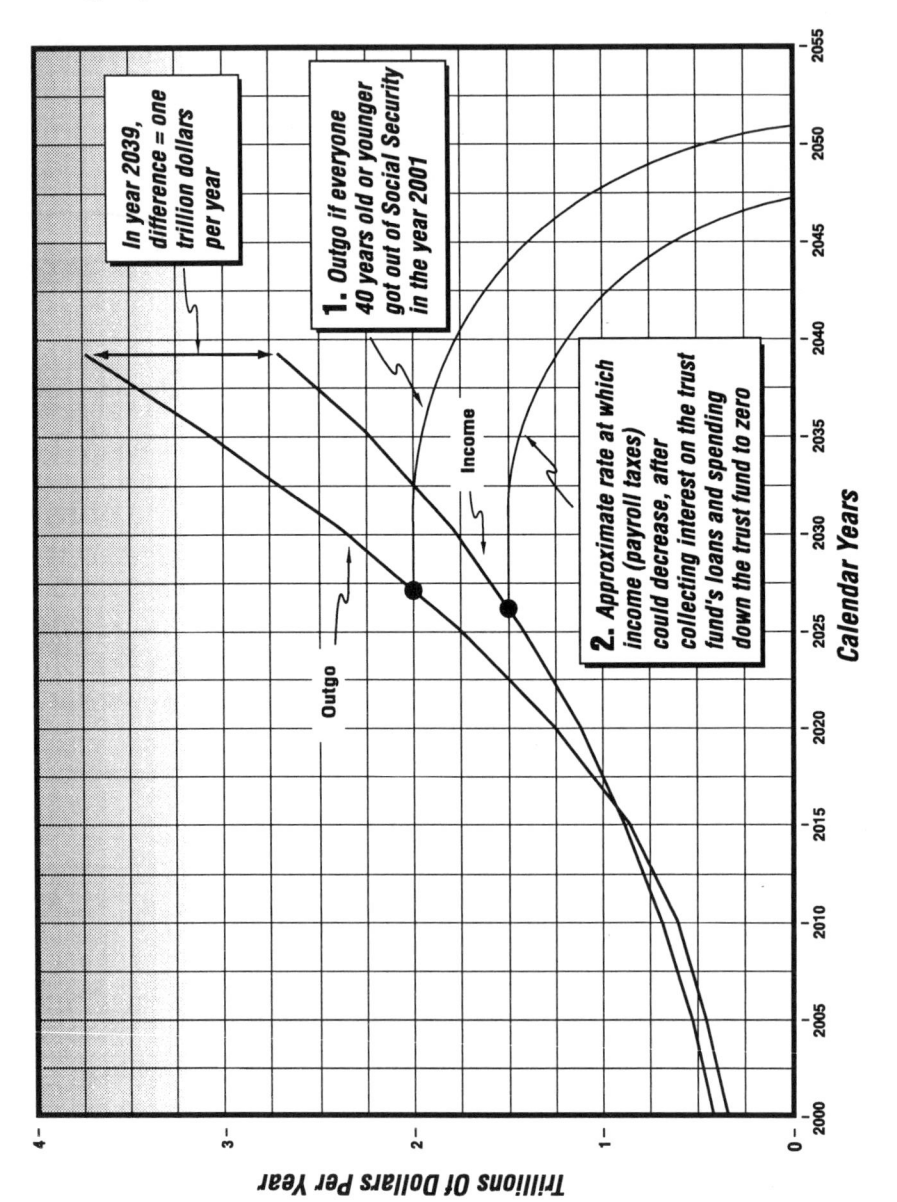

CHART 11-1: OASI (Retirement and Survivors Insurance) Only, for the calendar years 2000 through 2055, Cash Income (from payroll tax "contributions" and taxation of benefits, but excluding money from the trust fund and interest income owed to the fund by the U.S. Government) and Cash Outgo, per the Intermediate Forecast

have arrived, the checks will have to be written, and it will be too late.

This gives a particular urgency to doing something now and not procrastinating any longer. Using this ingredient of available time is the major factor in developing any solution.

The potential buildup of money in the trust fund

We need to say "potential," because any buildup of funds is only theoretical if Congress gets the money and spends it. But this buildup of funds can be another major ingredient in making any transition.

Just to review: Congress already owes the Social Security retirement trust fund about a trillion dollars. At present, this is only an IOU for the trust. If the IOU is to be collected, Congress needs to raise the money and pay the trust back. But the next 38 years are also a continuing problem, because the (intermediate) projection is that in those years the trust fund will take in another $50 trillion dollars, collect about $9-1/2 trillion dollars more in interest on the money that it is loaning out, and will see its balance rise to higher than $6 trillion, before paying out the last of $60 trillion and being gone (or, as the trustees say, "exhausted").

So there is a major, major issue here of whether all that money will be available for use by the Social Security retirement trust fund when it is time to write checks. If the money goes to or through Congress and doesn't all come back to the trust fund, then that adds to the problem.

Out of those three ingredients — the increasing deficit, the limited time until we have the surge of retirees, and the growing trust fund — we can put together solutions that achieve the balance we are after.

One such approach could be to take these three steps: (1) protect the Social Security trust funds from Congress, (2) offer

Saving Social Security (from Congress)

a privatization plan, and (3) frankly, raise payroll taxes for those who elect to stay with Social Security. The following explains each of those three steps.

Protecting the Social Security trust fund from Congress

The mandatory arrangement now is that any excess money in the Social Security retirement trust fund has to be "loaned" to Congress. In fact, they have always spent it all. But if they did have an excess, they could pass it on through and loan it out to the public. When Social Security needed its money back, Congress could then either develop surpluses of its own (out of which to pay the money back) or else borrow the money back from the public in order to turn around and pay it back to Social Security.

The problem with all of this is that it runs the money through the greedy hands of Congress, accomplishing nothing constructive, making everything very confusing, and making possible much that is not helpful to the trust fund.

All of these problems could be avoided by changing the law so as to keep the money out of Congress's hands. First, have them repay what they already owe. Secondly, none of the Social Security money would ever go to them in the future. Third, make Social Security truly independent of Congress, with its own bank accounts. And fourth, the Social Security retirement trust fund would loan any of its excess funds directly to the public itself, so it collected real interest income directly.

In other words, get Congress out of the act. Never let the money go to or through Congress. Don't ask them to reform. Just take the money away from them.

The excess money in the Social Security trust fund would not be "invested in the stock market." The excess money would be used to buy bonds, not stocks. The earnings on these bonds (which would be *real* bonds, not the phony *special* bonds used now as IOUs from Congress) would be presumably at the market rate now being charged to Congress. But the interest income on the bonds would be real cash, not an IOU from Congress.

If the trillions of dollars presently expected to come into the Social Security retirement trust fund from the already-increased payroll taxes can in fact be protected and kept available for its originally-intended purpose (and which would cover the retirees' needs through 2039), this would be major step #1 in making any transition and in really solving the problems.

With reference again to Chart 11-1, the money coming from repayment from Congress and from interest income was going to fill that gap between the two lines until the year 2039. (After that, nothing would fill the gap). But if that money that was going to fill that *upward*-moving gap is instead used to fill the *downward*-moving gap, it will have been the key to turning this situation around and solving it.

Offering a 10% privatization option (and assuming that all below 40 will take that option)

A second part of any solution would be to offer a privatization plan that would aim to provide enough incentive that everyone below the age of 40 would elect to leave the Social Security plan and thereafter fund their own retirements.

Of course, not everyone under 40 would elect to leave Social Security. But some over 40 who have higher earnings would also elect to leave. For now, we are going to do some calculations that assume the maximum: that essentially everyone under 40 does elect to leave Social Security.

The liabilities of the trust fund end when the last retiree on the plan dies. If (for our example) this plan is introduced and accepted and no one under 40 is now in the Social Security retirement plan, that means that the 40 years olds will live maybe on average for another 50 years, and that after that (after about 2051), there will be no remaining liability. The liability is over in 50 years. That objective would have been accomplished by about the year 2051.

On Chart 11-1, page 198, this elimination of the outgos of the fund is represented by the line that starts (about in the middle of the chart) from the present outgo line and instead curves downward to the right until it ends in the year 2051 (or thereabouts). This line starts in about 2027 (when those who are presently 40 become 66 or 67 and are the last ones to retire and start drawing Social Security) and goes down until about 2051, when the last of them are around 90.

Do note how much higher up the present outgo line this new downward-curving line would have had to start *if the plan didn't start until 5 years later!* Trace on up that top outgo line to the year 2032, and *then* start trying to draw a downward-curving line. You can see that by then the problem has gotten much larger, making the solution take much longer (if it isn't, in fact, too late).

There is probably not a lot of doubt that the incentives could work, and nearly all of those under the age of 40 would leave Social Security. That *would* eliminate this future liability, at least getting us that far toward a solution.

That then moves us to the third part of the solution, and the way in which we can put all of this together.

Temporarily increasing payroll taxes for those who stay with Social Security

The problems of the present Social Security retirement income system didn't develop overnight, and it is reasonable to expect that it will take 50 years or so to solve them. But whatever we work out has to solve the problem, not just keep passing it along to our children and grandchildren to pay for later.

Those of us who are retired or who are near retirement can expect to receive far, far more in benefits than we ourselves ever paid in payroll taxes. The system has simply evolved that way, with the politicians voting more and more benefits for the politically active retirees. We are also living to collect benefits for many more years than were originally expected. But now we have come to the point where it is dawning on everyone that there aren't going to be enough kids coming along to pay for all the benefits that have been voted for all the increasing number of seniors.

The younger workers who understand this situation see no sense in continuing to pay a payroll tax that sustains a Social Security system that is predicted, even by the trustees themselves, to be unable to continue. They know they could do better by investing the money for themselves, instead of putting it into the payroll tax.

However, they need to remember that, contrary to what they may have been led to believe, they have not been paying payroll taxes as a savings plan for their *own* retirements. No, they have been paying for the retirement income of their parents, their grandparents, great-grandparents and their peers. So what each of them paid was not for themselves but for someone else.

So if these younger workers leave the Social Security retirement income system, they should simply be happy that they got out, that they no longer will be required to pay into something from which they will most likely get nothing. But they shouldn't be asking for some refund or credit for what they have paid to date. They may have paid in a considerable amount, but that is what they are giving up.

On the other hand, those who are staying in the Social Security retirement system and who are not yet retired, need to acknowledge that the present plan is a very good bargain for them. So they are going to need to pay some slightly increased payroll taxes in those years until they *do* retire. Why shouldn't they? Were they really expecting a free ride? Would *that* have been fair?

If we are going to achieve the balance necessary to solve this Social Security retirement income problem, we need to all start thinking of ourselves more as responsible parties, rather than as victims (particularly when we are *not* victims).

Until the great majority of us come around to that point of view, all of the arithmetic in the world isn't going to bring us to a resolution of the problem. We're all going to have to "give a little," not expecting "someone else" (particularly our children and grandchildren) to do all the giving.

But let's do go through the arithmetic of the plan proposed here.

To review, we are starting from a present situation where the typical employee has 5.3% of taxable income taken out as payroll tax for the OASI (Social Security retirement and survivors "insurance" system), with the employer then also being taxed for another 5.3%. A total of 10.6% of taxable payroll.

This proposal would leave the *employer's* 5.3% tax alone for the next 25 years. That tax would stay at 5.3% until the year 2027, at which time it would come down to 5.0% and start coming down thereafter by 0.5% (half of one percent) every two years until there was no longer any tax on the employer for OASI starting in the year 2047. The employer would not have to pay an increased payroll tax. The employer's part of the tax would start going down in 2027, at the same time that the tax would also start going down for the employee.

The increase in the payroll tax would be on only the employee, not the employer. The payroll tax would go up 2.0% immediately and then gradually over the next 25 years, essentially going up in line with the increasing costs. Then in the year

2027, the payroll tax rate would start dropping at a rate of roughly 1% every two years until there was also no OASI tax for the *employee* in the year 2047.

There would be no need for further Social Security retirement income (OASI) payroll taxes starting in the year 2047. The fund would have enough money left to pay out the remaining small obligations to those still drawing Social Security in their 90's or older.

The exact proposed schedule is shown in Table 11-1 on page 207. This schedule shows that all who elect to stay with Social Security could expect to have their payroll taxes go up by 2.0% of their taxable income immediately. Thereafter, there would be increases of 0.7% (7/10ths of one percent) roughly every 5 years, until the payroll tax, coming out of the employee's pay, has gone up from its present 5.3% to 10.8%. That transition happens over the next 25 years. And no sooner does the tax get up to that level than it soon thereafter starts heading down toward zero.

But would that payroll tax increase really make up for all the income that would be lost when the younger workers dropped out of the Social Security retirement plan?

For one thing, there are excessive amounts of payroll tax being charged right now, building up the trust fund, so it can be available to cover any transition.

More importantly, though, we need to look a little more closely at how much payroll tax would actually be lost if those under 40 all went on their own. Start off by thinking of a workforce with ages between 18 and 39 and between 40 and 70. Those in that younger 22-year age span (18 through 39) are going to be making a lot less money than those older workers in the 30-year age span (from 40 to retirement). Not only does the older group make more money, but there are more of them.

Let's assume for now that about one third of the payroll tax comes from the younger group and two thirds of it comes from

TABLE 11-1

Proposed OASI Payroll Tax

Year	Change	Employee	Change	Employer	Total	Total Change
2000	0	5.3%	0	5.3%	10.6%	0
2001	+2.0%	7.3%	0	5.3%	12.6%	+2.0%
2005	+0.7%	8.0%	0	5.3%	13.3%	+2.7%
2010	+0.7%	8.7%	0	5.3%	14.0%	+3.4%
2015	+0.7%	9.4%	0	5.3%	14.7%	+4.1%
2020	+0.7%	10.1%	0	5.3%	15.4%	+4.8%
2025	+0.7%	10.8%	0	5.3%	16.1%	+5.5%
2027	-0.8%	10.0%	-0.3%	5.0%	15.0%	+4.4%
2029	-1.0%	9.0%	-0.5%	4.5%	13.5%	+2.9%
2031	-1.0%	8.0%	-0.5%	4.0%	12.0%	+1.4%
2033	-1.0%	7.0%	-0.5%	3.5%	10.5%	-0.1%
2035	-1.0%	6.0%	-0.5%	3.0%	9.0%	-1.6%
2037	-1.0%	5.0%	-0.5%	2.5%	7.5%	-3.1%
2039	-1.0%	4.0%	-0.5%	2.0%	6.0%	-4.6%
2041	-1.0%	3.0%	-0.5%	1.5%	4.5%	-6.1%
2043	-1.0%	2.0%	-0.5%	1.0%	3.0%	-7.6%
2045	-1.0%	1.0%	-0.5%	0.5%	1.5%	-9.1%
2047	-1.0%	0.0%	-0.5%	0.0%	0.0%	-10.6%

the older group. But the payroll tax paid by the *employer* is not going to change. So the net result would be that the expected (total 10.3%) payroll tax would be lost on only one half of one third of the taxable payroll. In other words, 1/6 of the total payroll tax income would be lost, to begin with, if all workers under 40 dropped out of the Social Security plan.

As the years go on, however, this younger group of workers on whom the payroll tax is being paid by only their employers will become a greater and greater percent of the total workforce, until by around the year 2027 or so they will have (1) become *all* of the workforce and will have (2) all retired. From the standpoint of the arithmetic, this means that over those 27 years or so the lost income will increase steadily from being about 1/6 of the payroll tax income to being 1/2 of it. (Through those years, the employer would still be paying the 5.3%).

For all of those reasons, the proposed gradual increase in the payroll tax rate for those who remain with Social Security should compensate for the expected gradual decrease in the payroll tax income from those who left.

The power of the Social Security actuaries' computers can be harnessed to come up with far more sophisticated numbers and combinations. For now, the purpose is simply to show how a solution is possible – a solution that does not pass the cost on in the form of debt that our children and grandchildren have to pay.

The general explanation, once more, is that those who are going to get the benefits need to accept a greater responsibility to pay their own bill. They will still get a very good deal.

In summary

We have to work this out so we achieve a balance among present workers and retirees and do not leave the bill for our children and grandchildren to pay.

The ingredients that we have to work with in reaching a solution are (1) the escalating deficit expected in the Social Security retirement income fund, (2) the time left until the number of retirees surges, and (3) the potential buildup of dollars in the trust fund as a result of present payroll taxes.

The solution can come from a combination of (1) protecting the Social Security trust fund money from Congress, (2) offering a 10% privatization option that all those generally below the age of 40 will accept in exchange for leaving the Social Security retirement plan, and (3) temporarily increasing payroll taxes for those who stay with the Social Security retirement plan.

After that payroll tax increase and the retirement of those who are now 40, payroll taxes (paid by both employer and employee) for retirement would head steadily down to zero and be eliminated. And there would be no debt left for our children and grandchildren to pay.

Those who think these solutions are unacceptable or unreasonable are given the challenge to come up with better solutions, as long as these alternative plans (1) accept responsibility for solving the problem among the present workers and retirees and (2) achieve a balance among them.

Solutions _are_ possible. But there is a window of opportunity that is closing quickly, unless we do something right now. You know enough by now to understand that time really is running out.

Question #12

So, In Summary, What Are Our Options?

Hopefully, you know a lot more now than you did a short time ago. You are full of new information, but the question is now what to do with it all. This leads to the need to figure out what the options are.

In other words, without picking one at this point, what are all the possible ways in which we could solve the retirement income problem? Also, for those who want to consider privatization, there are quite a few options for any such plan.

We can start off by making a list of all the real options for solving the problems of the present Social Security retirement income plan. Some of these clearly are not going to work, but someone is certain to suggest them, so we do need to make a thorough list.

Procrastinate

#1. The first option will be to do what we have been doing for years: procrastinate some more. We can say that we need more information before we can decide. One continuing major way out is to question any and all projections of the future. The actuarial assumptions may be high or low. We may grow our way out of this. Who knows what the future will bring, or whether the information is right or wrong? We can claim that it is all just too confusing or indefinite. Wait and see.

Or we can decide that we aren't ready to bite the bullet or face the pain. Politicians may not want to face pain or fiscal reality, because they don't think their constituents are ready for it. Why choose some definite pain now, when there is the possibility of either none of it or lots of it later on someone else's watch? Stalling or buying time will definitely come up as a main possibility.

The main argument against further procrastination will of course be the present Social Security surplus, the fact that it ceases in about a decade, and the inescapable facts of demography: the way that many millions of us will be retiring soon with not nearly as many millions being added to the workforce.

There are clear advantages in acting now, rather than procrastinating. If we wait and let the cash get away, it may be impossible to get that cash back so we have it to pay retirement checks. Timing really is very important to a solution.

"Solutions" that don't really solve the problems

#2. Another option will be to arrive at compromise "solutions" that don't solve the problems. This has also been the option that was selected in the past. Out of plain old fear, agreement is reached to do something that everyone knows doesn't really take care of the future, but which at least gets us through the present. We find a way to tiptoe away from the problem and to claim that we have solved it, when we haven't.

As you know by now, the most likely form for such a "solution" will be to, in one way or another, escape the costs of what we want by borrowing the money and leaving the bill to our children, grandchildren, or those yet to be born.

Hopefully, we will face up to our national responsibility to not select this option.

Changing benefits

#3. A third option might be to change benefits. One of our original ground rules was that we wouldn't get into this. It may come up as a separate issue, such as to correct the ways in which the present benefit structure favors those who are married. If it is no great distraction to make such changes, fine. One question, though, would be whether any change is adding costs to an already overloaded system.

Increasing the "special bond" interest rate

#4. There are people who will bring this up as a fourth option, but you should know by now that this is a phony solution. Any such "rate" increase would be simply a way to put an artificial surcharge on Congress, with that additional money having to come from further income tax increases. Beyond that, Congress isn't even paying the *regular* interest rate on its borrowing and never has. Congress just pays with IOUs. This surcharge would just be a sneaky way to pull income tax revenue over into the Social Security fund (assuming, of course, that Congress paid both the basic interest rate *and* the phony add-on charge).

Earmarking part of "the surplus" for Social Security

#5. This will come up as a fifth option, but you ought to be on to this one by now, too. To begin with, which "surplus" are we talking about? As long as the Social Security surplus is mixed up with the surplus (or deficit) of Congress's own governmental operations, it is hard or impossible to know what surplus it is and where it is coming from.

When a politician says he is using "the surplus," or some percentage or allocation of "the surplus," to "save Social Security," the first things to remember are that (1) Social Security is running a surplus now, (2) by present law it can't do anything but give that money to Congress, (3) so there is no way that Congress *can* be paying anything *back!*, and (4) Congress claims the Social Security surplus as a part of its own surplus in "the" budget. It's a mandatory one-way street. If Congress has any money coming in from the Social Security trust fund that it doesn't spend, or if it actually has a surplus in its own operations –two *enormous* "ifs" — the money has to go to pay down the public debt.

When members of Congress say they are allocating money to "save Social Security," all they can really be suggesting (prematurely and indirectly) is that by paying down the public debt now, they will be more *able* to — and actually *might* — some time *in the future* — borrow *back* from the public and (not spend that money but) actually pass it on through to Social Security as repayment of what Congress owes the trust fund when the trust fund is not running a surplus of its own and *does* need its money back.

(If you can't follow all of that, you understand why the accounting of Social Security needs to be separated from that of the rest of the government!)

This "allocation of the surplus" business is all politics or speculation, and not a real solution for now. To *really* get money back to the Social Security trust fund is another option, and a real one, that is further down this list.

Cost reduction

#6. A sixth option will be to somehow reduce the expected future costs of Social Security. That can be done basically three ways.

The first and by far the largest way to reduce costs would be to somehow convince those who are presently on their way to becoming future liabilities (checks to be paid out) of the Social Security retirement plan that they should drop out of the plan and *not* become future costs for the plan. In other words, by full privatization.

The second would be to reduce the benefits of those who do remain with the Social Security retirement plan. The hue and cry has been, "Absolutely impossible!! No way!! Never!! Political suicide!!"

But those claims may have been made by people who really didn't understand the problem. These people didn't understand that staying with the present plan is already *going to* result in a reduction of benefits, unless something changes in a major way. And there can be a differentiation made between those already drawing benefits and those who have yet to start drawing benefits.

One way in which some plans propose to reduce the benefits of the present Social Security plan is disguised by the words "adjusting the bend points." To begin with, "adjusting" means reducing, and in some of the major plans it means reducing some of the benefits by about 1/3. The "bend points" are part of the formula used to figure out the monthly benefits that retirees will receive.

When a person retires, the calculation of benefits starts with the "AIME" (average indexed monthly earnings), with "indexed" meaning that the earnings history (presently over 35 years) is adjusted for inflation. The "AIME" then becomes the basis of calculating what monthly benefit the retiree will start receiving. The calculation is done by multiplying the AIME times three "bend points."

The first part of the benefit will be 90% of the first part of the AIME (presently just over $500/month, and increasing each year to adjust to inflation). The second part of the benefit will be 32%

of the next part of the AIME (such as, presently, from about $500 to $3000/month). And the third part of the benefit will be 15% of everything above that (presently, everything over about $3,000/month).

The three "bend points" are presently 90%, 32%, and 15%. So if a plan proposes to "adjust" these bend points by multiplying the top two bend points (the 32% and 15%) by 98% each year for the next 20 years, that means that the benefits for those who have most of their earnings in the 90% category won't be affected much. But the benefits received from anything more than those minimal earnings will be cut by about a third. For example, if the 32% is reduced by 2% a year for 20 years, it becomes 21%. And if the 15% is reduced by 2% a year for 20 years, it becomes 10%.

So "adjusting the bend points" means cutting the Social Security benefits of those who make more than minimal incomes.

For example, the calculation in 1999 would be as shown at the left, but would be as shown on the right if the bend points had been reduced to 21% and 10%, for someone with an AIME of $5,000:

	Present bend points	Bend points proposed by some
First $505 x	90% = $ 454.50	90% = $ 454.50
$505 to $3,043 x	32% = 812.16	21% = 532.98
All over $3,043 x	15% = 293.55	10% = 195.70
Total	$1560.21	$1183.18

But the reduction of benefits *does* have to at least be put on the list of options. Or, more accurately, the present plan has *already* put this on the list, not as an option but as an expected fact.

The third way to reduce costs of the present plan would be to increase the normal retirement age (NRA) at which payment of full benefits starts, and/or the early retirement date at which payment of reduced benefits starts. This would be a continuation of an increase in these dates that has already started, would acknowledge the way in which life expectancies have increased greatly since the days when Social Security started, and could be done in a way that gives many years of advance warning, so people can have time to prepare for this change. Not reducing benefits, but just waiting a little longer before receiving them.

As Alan Greenspan, Chairman of the Federal Reserve Board, testified in 1997 before the U.S. Senate Task Force on Social Security of the Committee on the Budget, "… some delaying of the age of eligibility for retirement benefits is becoming increasingly pressing. For example, adjusting the full-benefits retirement age further to keep pace with increases in life expectancy in a way that would keep the ratio of retirement years to expected life span approximately constant would significantly narrow the funding gap."

Increases in payroll tax income

#7. The seventh option is the one that has been used the most, and therefore is probably mostly exhausted. That is to find ways to increase income into the Social Security retirement plan.

This has been done over the years by bringing more and more people into the program, with the intent of getting the payroll taxes of these people. The problems are that there are hardly any more people to round up and bring in, and that the people who have been brought in, in the past, are now going to be retiring and drawing benefits. This works for a while, but then has a reverse effect. At first it is a solution, because there is payroll income tax from these added people. But then it just becomes more of the same problem, when these people also retire and need retirement income.

Another way of increasing income for the present Social Security retirement plan has been to either increase the payroll tax rate or to increase the dollars of annual taxable income to which it applies. So that rate has gone up and up, and now covers all income to more than $80,000 a year, with that cap going on up each year. In effect, the increased payroll tax income is coming from those who make more money, although this doesn't result in any more benefits for them.

Another twist on this approach is to recommend that the payroll tax rate be increased only for the *employer*, thus making it more acceptable to the employees.

The real problem with these approaches, though, is that the forecasts by the Social Security trustees show that payroll taxes could be increased and increased, up to 25% or 44% of payroll, or more, and the costs (of Social Security and Medicare) will *still* be increasing. In other words, this amounts to chasing up a dead end street.

Raising payroll taxes, even to impossible percentages of total payroll, isn't going to solve the problems, particularly when we are heading toward having 2 or less workers per retiree.

Nevertheless, raising payroll taxes temporarily or for limited transitional purposes may be one option to consider.

Using income taxes to finance Social Security

#8. Another option that will come up will be to use income taxes (in addition to payroll taxes) as a means of financing the Social Security needs.

The traditional idea, however, has been to provide for Social Security (and later, Medicare), not through income taxes but through payroll taxes. From the beginning, President Roosevelt said Social Security should be self-sustaining "... in the sense that funds for payment of insurance benefits should not come from the proceeds of general taxation."

The intent has always been that payroll taxes would finance Social Security and only Social Security, and that income taxes would finance the rest of the government and only the rest of the government.

But the way in which the money has flowed from the Social Security trust fund and into the general treasury accounts, where Congress could spend it, rather than raising income taxes to pay its own bills, has confused things. It also muddied the waters recently to have Congress apply the income tax to Social Security benefits, with that income tax revenue then sent back to the Social Security trust fund.

This option will need to be discussed, but it should be very clear as to which bills are being paid and therefore who should be paying them. The preferable approach should be that Congress pays its own bills with income taxation, and Social Security meets its obligations with payroll taxes, and the two are kept separate.

Congress paying Social Security back

#9. Another option is to get Congress to pay back to the Social Security trust funds those amounts that it has borrowed, or that it owes as interest expense on that borrowing, and then to keep Congress from having access to the Social Security trust funds.

When we are told that there are no problems until the year 2037 and then someone else says the problem starts by the year 2015, the difference between those two years is the amount that Congress has borrowed, or might borrow in addition, or owes as interest on its borrowing. The problem is that Congress has never yet paid back anything to Social Security and that they show no prospects of ever being able to pay back.

So Congress is a big part of the problem, and will continue to be a big part of the problem until this option is dealt with. But in order to make this option possible, the laws will have to be changed to allow Social Security to loan its excess funds elsewhere, other than just to Congress, and to earn interest from some source other than Congress.

Separating Social Security from Congress

#10. A tenth option, related to the ninth one, is to separate Social Security entirely from Congress, not only in the accounting but also in the handling of the money. Under this option, not only could the public get a better picture of what is actually going on in these two separate organizations (instead of having it all lumped together, in one confusing total). But the public could also be sure that the Social Security money was staying in the Social Security organization, with Congress never even having access to it.

This is certainly an option that has to be considered seriously, especially when we see the problems that we have gotten into by *not* having Social Security truly separate and independent from Congress.

Means testing

#11. Another option would be to make Social Security "means tested." In other words, rather than having Social Security benefits go to everyone who has paid into the plan, the plan would become straight welfare, with the benefits going to only those without adequate "means" to provide for their own retirement. This would turn Social Security into an open transfer of wealth from all who pay in to only those who are poor or not well off.

Going this way would certainly cut the costs of the Social

So, In Summary, What Are Our Options? 221

GRIN AND BEAR IT

"I believe most congressmen are decent people ... they just can't be trusted with money."

Security retirement income plan, but is such a major change in the purpose of the plan that it can be considered as essentially a dead idea before it even gets brought up. But it *will* come up as an option.

Reducing the CPI (cost of living) index

#12. A twelfth option would be to reevaluate the cost of living (CPI) index, in order to be sure that it doesn't overstate the inflation rate and therefore to be sure that this index isn't being used to raise Social Security benefits each year more than they should be raised.

When this issue was brought up a few years ago, in reference to solving the problems of Social Security, it caused a big political stink, and was supposedly dropped. But in fact, after that, academic review of the CPI went on, and some changes were made. In any case, it should be an academic issue, settled on a rational basis. The index should be corrected, if necessary, to be sure it measures "inflation" accurately (if that is even possible to determine), not because we need it reduced as a means of keeping Social Security costs down.

This option will come up as a means of reducing the costs of Social Security, but it should be handled quite separately, out of the hands of the politicians. Beside that, it is almost irrelevant as any real contribution to the solution of the real problems of Social Security.

Getting market returns on invested money

#13. A very important option is to somehow obtain market returns on money that is saved and held for future retirement purposes. In other words, how can the money be invested, so it really *earns*, instead of just being spent? The basic option here is whether the government or the individual should do the investing.

President Clinton brought up the proposal that government do the investing, and it was quickly vetoed, for a great number of reasons. But there may well be a role for investing, not by the Congress-controlled government, but by the Social Security trust fund, *if* that trust fund is truly under independent management and especially if that trust fund's investing were to be for only a transitional period, as we moved toward privately-controlled investment.

Also, the purchase of *bonds* in the market should not bring up the control issues that might still be involved with Social Security's buying and owning the voting shares of company *stocks*.

Individuals clearly can get the advantages of compounding through their own investments, and that option is therefore of course the one that is receiving so much attention as the natural answer.

Hybrid Social Security/investment plans

#14. A final option would be for some hybrid mix of investment and the present Social Security plan. There are typically complicated provisions that the return of the invested part will be compared somehow to the Social Security benefits, and Social Security will "make up the difference." Or the "personal" accounts will be "privately owned but publicly managed."

One thing to think through on any of these plans that "make up the difference" or which pay after some level or standard has been reached is how that "difference" will actually be calculated every year, 25 to 50 years from now. You might be sitting down, at age 79, around income tax time, filling out your additional government form on which you report (in total, for only these retirement income accounts) your dividend income and interest income, your capital gains and your capital loss carryforwards, the money you took out of the funds last year, or maybe some hypothetical annuity return off the year-end market value of your stock investments, bonds and other accounts, — so you could then compare it to what Social Security has notified you would otherwise have been your benefits that year, — so you would then know what "difference" to apply for. A lot of these plans sound fine in theory, until you start trying to figure out how they would actually work in the real world.

At this point, we are not talking about picking among the options, but just about making a list of and reviewing all the general options that might be brought up (even if some of the options don't make any sense at all).

In summary, the ones we have come up with for solving the problems of the Social Security retirement system are:

1. Procrastination.
2. Claiming we have solved the problem when we really haven't.
3. Changing benefits.
4. Increasing the "special bond" interest rate charged to Congress.
5. Earmarking part of "the surplus" for Social Security.
6. Cutting the future costs of Social Security, probably by (a) getting people to leave the plan, (b) reducing benefits, or (c) increasing normal and/or early retirement dates.
7. Increasing the future payroll tax income of Social Security, by ways such as bringing more people into the plan or raising payroll tax rates or caps on the amount of income to which the rates are applied.
8. Using income taxes (in addition to payroll taxes) to finance Social Security.
9. Making Congress pay back what it owes Social Security and then not borrow any more.
10. Separating Social Security from the control of Congress.
11. Changing Social Security to have it be "means tested."
12. Rechecking the accuracy of the CPI index, which is used to calculate the annual increases in Social Security benefits.
13. Somehow getting the advantages of compounding on the money that is saved for retirement purposes.
14. Hybrid Social Security/investment plans.

So, In Summary, What Are Our Options?

Maybe you can think of other options, but the above would seem to be it. If we are going to get to our goal, it will have to be down one of those roads, or down several of them. But those appear to be the only roads that can get us there.

It might be an interesting test of your knowledge at this point, though, to let you review a set of proposals of "The Way to Real Reform," made by the economists who wrote "Social Security – The Phony Crisis." Here are the proposals from their book:

1. Raising or lifting the cap on the payroll tax. "...it would undoubtedly provoke some backlash among upper-income taxpayers."
2. "A more politically palatable option would be to lift the cap on the employer's part of the tax."
3. "...it would make sense to supplement Social Security's payroll tax with a tax on nonlabor income. We would correct this mistake (of having dropped capital gains rates) by restoring the old capital gains tax rate and funneling the difference into the Social Security trust fund."
4. "... the Treasury could simply pay a higher rate of interest on the funds it borrows from the Social Security trust fund. Raising that rate from 6.3% to 9.3% would take care of about half of the projected 75-year deficit."
5. Reform other inequities, such as how women are heavily penalized for their time spent out of the workforce, although this reform would be more costly.
6. "If we feel a need to have the Social Security accounts balanced over a 75-year time horizon, that is a simple enough task to accomplish. President Clinton's proposal to put $2,800 billion of general revenue into the trust fund over the next 15 years eliminates almost half the projected shortfall."

They go on to conclude: "Rather than cutting our nation's

largest and most successful antipoverty program, we should extend the principles of universal social insurance to the area of health care. Medicare and Medicaid have taken us part of the way, but...social insurance holds the best promise of correcting the real nondemographic causes of our 'entitlement crisis' in the area of health care."

It is clear that there will be many options to consider and much to be sure we understand.

Privatization options

We then need to also address the main options that seem to be under consideration for those who would elect privatization and the investment of their own money.

There may be even more details, but at least 14 options are under consideration in designing a program of personal retirement accounts:

#1. What percent of pay can be set aside with tax deferral? The examples that you have seen suggest that 10% would work. Why not 12% or 14%? One concept is that these personal retirement accounts would be only for doing what the Social Security retirement system set out to do: be sure people at least had a minimum "floor" assurance of not retiring in poverty. For savings in addition to this, we already have the IRAs and 401ks, which will presumably have less restrictions on them. Also, the government loses income tax revenue on every additional percent of income that is not taxed, so there has to be a balance between retirement savings incentives and the government's need for income tax revenue. Those who start early in life with a 10% set aside in a retirement savings account, and who achieve historical returns on what they invest, should retire with far, far more than any minimum "floor" amount.

#2. Should this (10%?) savings set aside be mandatory or optional? There will of course be the attraction of being able to defer taxation on any amounts set aside. People might be considered fools not to take advantage of this. But in fact some people, if given the option, will skip the savings opportunity in preference to immediate spending needs. Society's objective here is to make people do certain things (such as save for their own retirement) at least to the extent that these people are then not a burden on others in society. So the program has to be mandatory, at least up to some certain point.

But defining that point is difficult. At one extreme, there will be those who quite clearly have saved enough, or have enough money anyway, that there is no sense –from the standpoint of our not wanting them to become wards of the state— in making it mandatory that they save even more. The problem, then, is to determine the point at which people have saved enough that they can be allowed to opt out of further funding of their own personal retirement accounts. In so many words, at what point can we say to them, "It's now your responsibility, if you want to take it, but your choice says that *we* are no longer responsible for your income when you are retired."

The practical but difficult approach probably has to be for some minimum dollar amount to be saved (and left in the account to keep earning) before a person could sign such a release. That gets into complications, of course. It would depend on the person's age and income level at that time. It would have to be a minimum changed annually, and which allowed for the fact that the value of the account could fluctuate after the person opted out. One solution might be to say that the person would have to be at least 60 and have an account worth which would, in theory, buy an inflation-indexed annuity equal to half of an average person's recent earnings level.

There does need to be, though, some way for people to opt

out of this mandatory savings requirement if it has clearly accomplished its objective.

#3. Will credit be given somehow for past payroll taxes paid? Skipping over, for now, the difficulties of even calculating that amount, (and maybe even trying to give allowance for how inflation has changed those numbers over the years), the point has already been made that those payroll taxes clearly were paid for *someone else's* retirement, so there really is no rationale for giving any credit. Also, in trying to achieve balance, it can be said that this is something that those who opt out of Social Security are giving up. But the giving of such credit (possibly in the form of bonds, that can be cashed in at time of retirement) will come up as an option. The point needs to be made that it increases the cost of any transition enormously.

#4. Should survivors' insurance be mandatory or optional? If the personal retirement account coverage is to be comparable with what Social Security offered, then there needs to be coverage of survivors. However, in some people's cases, there *are* no potential survivors (that is, no spouse or children 18 or under). One simple option would be to require account holders to show continuing evidence that they have term insurance covering a spouse and any children under 18, and up to some minimum dollar amount. Term insurance, particularly early in life when account holders would most likely have children under 18, is extremely inexpensive. As life went on, if both a husband and wife were working and building their personal retirement accounts, a minimum level could be reached at which they were allowed to opt out of this coverage. And of course those who are single and without children would have no reason to have to incur the expense of this coverage. The coverage should be mandatory in only those circumstances where it is needed.

During retirement years, the coverage of the spouse can be through joint-and-survivor annuities or through the willing of balances to the spouse.

#5. Who is going to do the investing? Here, the options are basically either the government or the individual. There will probably be an unbelievable batch of mixed recommendations on this option. The simple solution will of course be for the government to establish parameters of safety and then to leave the choices to the individual.

#6. How limited should the investment choices be? This will be a question only if the decisions are going to be left up to individuals. Presumably, the choices will be a bit more restricted than those now allowed with IRAs or 401ks. But maybe not. The objective has to be safety, which will rule out investment in anything other than diversified middle-of-the-road selections that are going to essentially follow the market averages. Even that tight a range of selections would allow people to be very conservative (by putting all the money in the even safer but lower-paying bonds), or to take the risk of investment in stocks, or to elect a mix of bonds and stocks.

#7. Should investment by those who are married have to go in "shared accounts"? This is a proposal that is supposed to keep all the money from building up in the account of one spouse, to the possible detriment of the other spouse. First, there is a big administrative problem on "shared accounts," nice as the theory is. The wife works at one company, with its plan, and the husband works at another company, with its plan. If the sharing or splitting of the accumulating retirement money is a problem, it seems that this is something that should be worked out between the spouses, or by pre-nuptial agreements or by a divorce attorney, without the government requiring the pooling of what couples are earning. But this does come up as an option.

8. Will there or will there not be a guarantee that those who opt out of Social Security will at least get some minimum retirement benefit? This option is dangerous. The savings and loan fiasco is a good example. The S&Ls were "deregulated," and allowed to take on all sorts of risks, but were still insured by the government. They could take risks but still be protected from their risks. That unwise decision cost us, as taxpayers, only a few tens of billions of dollars.

The coverage of SSI (Supplemental Security Income) would still exist, as it does now for those who, for example, do not work enough to even generate an adequate retirement income from Social Security. But to start giving guarantees sets up a real danger that people will be attracted to take advantage of them. If you can fall back on the guarantee, why not go ahead and spend what you have and then collect on the guarantee too? At some levels of income, that will become an attractive option if there are guarantees. On the other hand, there may be a desire to use guarantees to sell privatization, as a means of assuring people that they will never need these guarantees anyway. One compromise might be guarantees limited to a certain amount and for only a certain number of years, but those might be little better than no guarantees at all. In any case, the offering of guarantees can set up conflicting objectives.

#9. Prior to retirement, could the funds be withdrawn for any of several worthy purposes, such as to buy a home, pay a major medical bill, or send the kids to college? The answer should clearly be "no." These funds must be strictly for the purpose for which they were saved. There might be some exception for medical bills in the case of terminal illness, or something like that, but in general it should be clear that these savings are for only one purpose.

#10. When can a person retire and start drawing from the account? Would it be correct that, "It's my money. I will retire when I decide to."? For one thing, there would be no need for some hard-and-fast rule that retirement must be at 65, or at 66 years and 4 months (as it is now, under Social Security), or even at 70. There would in fact be the flexibility for people to make their own decisions, based on their own savings, their own plans, and in fact their own assessment of how many years they have left.

But does the government dare let people make those decisions for themselves? Some of us are very concerned about that. And in fact some people would unfortunately retire too early, and/or spend their money too soon, or live longer than they expected, and end up running out of money. It's not a simple question. What is society's responsibility for those who, for one reason or another, end up in need?

One answer may be to establish a low minimum age, such as 60, at which a person can start taking money out of a personal retirement account. Or there can be a minimum number of years, such as 40, that there had to be money coming into the account. If workers started investing early, there could be little question that they would in 40 years or at age 60 have more than Social Security would have provided them.

With all these fears about income in their final years very active among retirees, the strong probability is that people will be sensible and conservative and won't take chances. Those with doubts will have chosen annuities. And SSI will still be there for those few who still end up in need. In a sense, we are back to the questions of responsibility and guarantees again.

#11. Should lump sum payouts be allowed at time of retirement? This question really brings the responsibility issue to a head. Should the retiree, for example, be able to take the money out of the personal retirement account (where it is tax deferred) and shift it over to an IRA, where there is more investment latitude but also the requirement for minimum annual payouts, starting at a certain age? How much are we going to let people take risks with their own retirement money, when society may get left with the responsibility for those who do not handle this risk successfully? This is another version of the options posed earlier and probably needs to be settled by believing in personal responsibility, while leaving the SSI backstop for the truly unfortunate. Any program that tries to make sure that essentially every retiree can "have his or her cake and eat it too" is simply impossible.

#12. Would all retirees be required to "annuitize"? That means, would they all have to buy annuities? One reason this idea comes up is that economists want to be able to compare with Social Security or be able to measure how much Social Security should "make up." It makes the calculation simple. But it is also an enormous restriction of personal freedom.

Some people, as a simple example, who know quite well that their family history or their personal health is such that they have fewer years than average left, would certainly be forced to come out as losers by having to buy annuities. They would be forced by the government rules to give their nest eggs to insurance companies in return for getting only a few years of income.

Those who want annuities to be mandatory are trying to achieve the objective of making sure that no one runs out of money in their retirement years. But to accomplish that objective for a few would also require being very restrictive on the great majority who do not need this protection and who would in fact suffer from having it.

If this is truly a person's own retirement money, accumulated because of the tax advantages given by the government, then the use of the money should be up to that person. Annuities should not be mandatory.

#13. Should there be a forced minimum annual payout from these funds after some age, (as there is for money in an IRA or a 401k)? Why *should* there be? These forced annual payouts are required in IRAs and 401ks basically for this reason: the government let you avoid taxation when you put the money in and on whatever it earned, but it doesn't want that money to escape taxation. So you have to take the money out so the government can get its tax on it. Your retirement income isn't the objective. Getting the tax to the government is. Congress needs the tax income.

Maybe some day we will have sales or consumption taxes, instead of income taxes, as a means of funding our federal government. But in the meantime, it would be nice if the need of our government for tax income were not to be the controlling factor in how we use our retirement savings. The preference on this option would clearly be that people be able to draw down their own personal retirement account balances as they see fit, not on some mandatory payout schedule that was set up just so the government could get its taxes.

#14. What will the tax treatment be for any balance left in the account at time of death (assuming that the money is to go to a surviving spouse or to children or others designated in a will)? This will be a subject for separate estate taxation laws, that hopefully will reward those who saved and invested diligently, in order to take personal responsibility for themselves, their spouses, their children, and their heirs.

There may be more options that will need to be considered

in designing the eventual personal retirement account plan. But the above discussion should certainly raise the essential issues.

Those working on the selection among these options can also get guidance from the experience of other already-existing large retirement savings plans, such as the federal government's own TSP (Thrift Savings Plan) and the very large college employees' TIAA-CREF retirement income plan. Excellent guidance can also come from Mr. José Piñera, of the International Center for Pension Reform, who can provide the experience of not only Chile but of the efforts of every country in the world dealing with these same problems.

We are now loaded with facts. We know our options. So how are we going to decide among all those options? This brings us to the subject of how we go about sorting all of this out.

Question #13

What Are the Principles, the Criteria that We Will Use to Decide among These Options?

We've already established many of the principles for decision-making when we decided, at the beginning, how we would work together to solve these problems.

We said our decisions had to be made seriously, soberly and with loving concern for all. That meant constant attention to "fairness, not favoritism." We are all called on to take our share of the responsibility. And we are again committing to sticking with it until we really *do* solve the problem of at least having a minimum retirement income for everyone, with continuing protection for survivors.

But as we get to actual decision-making time, we need to also reach agreement on the principles that we will use to sort out all of this information and the available options. Two people can look at exactly the same facts and options and come up with two entirely different solutions, because they operate on different principles.

So let's see how many such principles or criteria we can agree on.

Additionally, we need to agree...

... to KISS (keep it simple, stupid). The present disastrous state of affairs in our income tax system is the result of years and years of compromises and favoritism by Congress. If our Congress has to make the final decisions on a remodeling of Social Security, we need to make it clear to them that we want the answers to be clean and clear and simple, without a bunch of loopholes and complexities. One example of *not* keeping it simple would be to come up with a plan whereby some massive administration is needed, over many years in the future, to figure out how much each of us has set aside for our retirement income each year and then to possibly "make up the difference" between that and what the government had thought it might be able to pay each one of us. This may sound nice to some economists, but let's stay practical.

... that the Social Security retirement income program (OASI) is a big enough problem to tackle in itself, so any plans for change in the Disability Income (DI) or Medicare (HI) programs should be dealt with separately and later. This should be self-explanatory, but does at least need to be pointed out. The Social Security retirement income program is an enormous problem just in itself, and needs to be dealt with by itself.

... that SSI (Supplemental Security Income) will continue to provide a safety net for those with inadequate retirement income. This program should be left to do its job, and similarly Social Security does not need to be expanded in any way to take over this job. The safety net will remain.

... to reach solutions that last. The history of Social Security has been one of perpetual crises, which were taken care of by bandaids, until the patient had to again return to the

What Are the Principles, the Critia that We Will Use to Decide?

hospital. We need to agree to think it through well enough to do something different that really works this time.

... to encourage actual saving and investment in productive assets (usually in businesses), rather than spending. Here we get into the principles of what makes a nation's economy and standard of living great. Investment in productive assets is the key. The Social Security retirement plan has been based on spending, not investment.

... that we will solve this by "following the money," not by economic theory. These problems are not going to be solved by academic theoreticians who think the answers lie in modeling by stochastic simulation, restoring present-value-adjusted actuarial balances, contingent claims analysis, measuring economic well-being, option pricing theory, risk-adjusted interest rates, general equilibrium effects, macroeconomic consequences, the national savings rate, unfunded accrued liabilities, not diverting resources, standard money's worth calculations, differing risk characteristics, implicit or internal rates of return, utility gain, effects on the aggregate economy, regression equations, empirical evidence or any of the other lingo of the economists' trade. Some economists are happy when their theses prove that their abstract theories and algebraic formulas are as comprehensive as they are incomprehensible.

The problems of Social Security need to be worked out by people (including other economists) who work in terms of *cash*. People who talk in terms of money, payrolls, profit and loss. People who want to know where the cash is coming from, where the cash is, where the cash is going, what bills are going to be paid and from which cash. Accountants, not theoretical economists. The former deal with specifics and money, and the latter deal with generalities.

The solutions, for example, are not going to come from economists, such as those who wrote "Social Security, the Phony Crisis" and who refer to "... the relative insignificance of the economic impact of balancing the budget," or to "... non-issues like the national debt, the federal budget deficit, generational accounting, and the Social Security 'crisis'." They say, "The attention that has been devoted in recent years to the problem of balancing the federal budget...is also a good illustration of how the politics of non-issues has come to dominate civil society in the United States. Here is an economic policy that ... can only be regarded as trivial in its effects."

(They also, for that matter, refer to "the crass commercial interests of Wall Street" and "the gains of the War on Poverty.")

If might be worth noting too, that many members of Congress — particularly lawyers — may have had no more experience in these worlds of actual cash management than do some economists. They may be able to split hairs as well as the economists can, but get similarly lost in impractical theories and details.

The best example of how some economists deal in theory that is ungrounded in reality is their constant and blithe acceptance of the existence of "the trust fund." They theorize about how all that "money" or "value" will be used, (thereby proving their sloppy theories), without seeming to even realize in any way the fact that Congress has *spent* all that money that is supposed to be in that trust fund, and that it would require additional income tax in the billions or trillions to turn that value into actual *cash* that could be used to *pay* real retirement *checks*. Oh, those are just irrelevant real-world details for some economists.

It would have to be an economist, and not an accountant, who could "prove" that every two people working can pay all their own bills, and their children's bills, and still all by them-

What Are the Principles, the Critia that We Will Use to Decide? 239

selves, out of only their own cash, also fully support one retiree in Florida.

The solutions to Social Security have to be very clear about *cash*, where it comes from, where it is, where it goes. Nothing theoretical about it. If you don't understand the answers in those terms, then you need to keep asking for better explanations. "Show me the money! (not your theory)."

... that there needs to be an adequate transition time for changes that might adversely affect people. People could rightly be very upset about major changes being made so quickly that they had no chance to adjust. On the other hand, though, an immediate change is not like a change ten or twenty years from now, so we can of course defer changes at least long enough that people have a fair chance to adjust.

... that these problems didn't develop overnight, and that they are going to take many years to finally clean up. This doesn't mean that we can procrastinate about deciding what to do. Nor can we mix this principle up with a desire to pass the problems along to future generations. But we do in fact have to accept the idea that the decisions we make will take several decades in which to work out.

... about a need for balance between individual freedom and our responsibilities (through government) for each other. The preference should be for individual freedom to the maximum extent possible, with government responsibility kicking in only when individuals prove incapable of providing for themselves. The present Social Security system, by taxing such a large part of our income, in many ways actually makes it very difficult or even impossible for individuals to have enough money to do their own retirement saving. The government, in effect, preempts this responsibility from us.

There are very important basic principles at question here. Principles on which our nation was founded, for that matter. In candid terms, we may have a conflict of principle between those who believe in individual freedom and those who want a paternalistic welfare state.

... that the more freedom of choice there is, the better the plan. The best plan will allow those who wish to take personal responsibility for their retirement income to do that. Choice is a major value, and "opting out" of Social Security's retirement income plan should be an option for those who want to assume this responsibility themselves.

... to pay for what we expect to get. If we could really do that, much of the conflict about solving the Social Security retirement plan problems could cease quickly. Really settling these problems will in large part get down to whether people will accept the responsibility to pay their own bills, or whether they are really looking for a way to get someone else to pay them.

If our concerns are really for "the children," then a very specific way to express that concern will be to not send them the bill for our retirements.

We may well wish to add other principles or criteria that we use to reach our decisions. But with at least the above in mind, we can look at one possible set of conclusions as to what we should do.

Question #14

Then What Should We Do?

By now, you should be well enough informed that you can reach some conclusions of your own as to what we should do. But to at least finish this decision-making process with some sample answers, here we go.

First, we can go back to the list of options, go down that list, and eliminate the following options as choices we are not going to make:

1. Procrastination. This is the last thing to do, given the urgency of timing.
2. Claiming we have solved the problem when we really haven't.
3. Changing benefits. We said we wouldn't get into this.
4. Increasing the "special bond" interest rate charged to Congress. This is a phony solution, and actually would be a means of drawing income tax revenue into Social Security.
5. Earmarking part of "the surplus" for Social Security.
6. Cutting future costs of Social Security by reducing benefits. (But we *are* going to be trying to get younger people to leave the plan, and will be proposing changes in retirement dates).
7. No increases in future payroll taxes by bringing more people into the plan or by raising the amounts the tax rates are based on (any more than the amounts are scheduled to go

up anyway). (But some payroll tax rate increases will be proposed).
8. No use of income taxes to finance Social Security.

11. No means testing.
12. No rechecking of the accuracy of the CPI (cost of living) index.

14. No hybrid Social Security/investment plans. One or the other.

As we continue, it may also be worth mentioning again: there is no way to avoid risk. If you stay with Social Security, there is considerable risk. If you elect to leave Social Security and have your own personal retirement savings account, that is a risk too. Either way, risk. The following selections reflect a belief that the 75-year record of historical returns of the market will continue to be that good or better, and that there is therefore less risk in that alternative. The selections also reflect a belief that there is a major risk that the Social Security trustees' projections are correct, that the plan cannot continue to pay its promised benefits, and that the 60-year record of Congress's inability to ever create anything more than a small or temporary surplus of its own means that there is little chance that they will suddenly reform their ways and pay Social Security back.

Recommendations

The changes necessary to correct the problems of Social Security will have to be made by Congress and the President. But that brings up the additional problem, for the American public, of whether we can, in effect, get the fox (Congress) to give up custody of the henhouse (the Social Security trust fund). With Congress itself having an established record as being a major

Then What Should We Do?

"Our mistake was expecting the same people who got us into this mess to get us out."

part of the problem, there will need to be a very well-informed and insistent public demand for real reform, or Congress will not willingly give up its existing opportunity to spend Social Security funds.

The first solution to the problems of Social Security is to protect the Social Security (OASI) funds (past, present, and future) from Congress. So:

Recommendation #1: Continue and complete the process of separating Social Security entirely from the rest of the U.S. government, making it a truly independent agency. The trustees would no longer come from the Administration (the secretaries of Treasury, Labor, and Health and Human Services, etc.), but would be respected actual fiduciaries chosen from the financial community and given the real responsibility to protect the Social Security funds in behalf of present and future retirees. These trustees would be protected as much as possible, in the nature of appointments to the Federal Reserve Board.

The restriction that Social Security funds must be invested in only "special bonds" issued by the U.S. government would be removed, and in fact replaced with a restriction that the trustees are to hereafter *not* invest in such bonds. In other words, Social Security would no longer be able to loan any excess cash to the government, where Congress could spend it. To the contrary, the trustees would have the responsibility to invest the trust funds directly in the market, presumably almost entirely in actual bonds, so that this money earns real interest income that is actually paid directly into the Social Security fund. Congress would have no say whatsoever in these investment decisions. These decisions would be the exclusive responsibility of the trustees.

This would all, of course, require legislation, but is absolutely and completely possible.

The major advantage, indeed the necessity, is that such a change keeps the income of the Social Security fund from ever being under the control of Congress. Congress has proven itself to be an untrustworthy debtor, but we would not hereafter need to be concerned as to whether they would reform or not. This change would take the decision away from them, and possibly thereby encourage them to focus more on their lack-of-a-real-surplus-of-our-own problems, which they need to do in order to pay Social Security back.

Another advantage relates to the question of who pays which taxes. If the financing of the Social Security retirement program is isolated within the Social Security Administration, then the income is going to be *payroll* taxes, which come from society in a much different distribution than do *income* taxes. However, if we instead look to the federal government to be the source of the needed funds, that means not *payroll* taxes, but *income* taxes, which are not paid proportionately by the same people. In principal, if the payroll tax is meant to pay the retirement income, then that income from *payroll* taxation needs to be kept within Social Security and, for that matter, be increased or decreased in order to meet the needed obligations of Social Security *without* getting *income* taxation involved.

Recommendation #2: This recommendation follows from the first recommendation, and it is that Congress be directed to (a) pay interest income to the Social Security fund *in cash* (not just with more IOUs) on those amounts (about a trillion dollars) that it has already borrowed from the fund, and also to (b) establish a program of repaying that trillion dollars of principal to Social Security.

In other words, Congress needs to be required to pay back what it has borrowed from Social Security. It can do that only by (a) having a surplus in its own books (that means, income in excess of outgo, or outgo less than income) and then using those funds to pay its debts to Social Security, or (b) borrowing more from the public and using that to pass through to Social Security to pay off *that* borrowing.

But one way or another, the sooner Social Security can get its own money back from Congress, the sooner we can get the responsibilities of these two organizations ("the company" — on-budget — and "the retirement plan" — off-budget) totally separated.

To go back and put it all in "Mary and Harry" terms, we might wrap up that story this way:

Mary told him, "Harry, I've had it with you! It's all over. I'm *outta* here! I'm not supporting your habit any more. I'm getting a separate account in a separate bank. From here on, I collect my payroll taxes and pay only *my* bills. You need to get your act together and start living within your *own* income. You can collect your *income* taxes and do two things. First, you pay *me* back. Second, you pay your *own* bills!"

Recommendation #3 follows: The President must hereafter present "THE Budget" for his government (the "On-Budget" part) as just that, with Social Security never included in it again. Congress will thereafter be required to talk about "the" budget as just that, and about any "surplus" as actually their own, not distorted by Social Security income. Separately, the Social Security trustees would continue to issue *their* annual reports, and can be much more candid in stating the fiscal realities of the fund. If Congress, for example, starts considering legislation to increase benefits without facing up to the related costs, the trustees will now be independent enough that they can object, "loud and clear," because they are now separate from the Administration and being looked to as truly responsible, separate fiduciaries of the nation's retirement funds.

This third recommendation is, in a sense, only a statement that Congress and the President should actually do what they said they should do earlier: actually get Social Security OFF-budget. OUT of the budget. Separate. Forever. The retirement plan run by honestly independent trustees, on one set of accounting books, with separate bank accounts. The "company" run by its separate management, with its own "profit and loss" statement.

Next, we need one change, and then one agreement to *not* make a change, in the legislation that determines the income and outgo of the Social Security retirement fund:

Recommendation #4: In recognition of the clear increase in life expectancy that has happened during the life of Social Security, three further changes need to be made in retirement dates.

The first such change would be to keep moving the NRA (normal retirement age) up from age 67 to age 70, as shown in column 4 of Table 14-1. Column 3 shows the present schedule, column 4 shows the proposed new schedule, and column 5 shows how much longer a person would need to wait (under the proposed new schedule) to start normal full retirement.

For example, someone born in 1951 (and therefore now 50 years old) has an NRA now of age 66. Under the proposed new plan, that person's NRA would be 67 years and 4 months, or 1 year and 4 months later. That would be an 8% increase in the time until the NRA, and there would be no change until 16 years from now.

Or, to show the amount of change for several different ages:

Year you were born	Your age now	Years until your NRA on the present plan	Time Added on new plan	Percent increase
1946	55	11	6 mos.	+5%
1951	50	16	1 yr 4 mos.	+8%
1956	45	21 yrs, 4 mos.	1 yr 10 mos.	+9%
1961	40	27	2 years	+7%
1966	35	32	2 yrs 10 mos.	+9%

This says, for example, that if you are now 55, no change would affect you for the next 11 years. But 11 years from now, your normal retirement date would be six months later (11 years and 6 months from now). In 11 years, you wait 6 months more. Instead of waiting 11 years to retire, you wait 11 years and 6 months, that being 5% longer.

TABLE 14-1: Recommended Changes in Normal and Early Retirement Ages

1. Year You Were Born	2. Year You'll Be 65	3. NRA Now	4. New NRA	5. You Wait This Much Longer	6. You Are This Old in 2001	7. Earliest Possible Benefits Now	8. Earliest Possible Proposed	9. You Wait This Much Longer
1936	2001	65	65	0	65	62	62	0
1937	2002	65	65	0	64	62	62	0
1938	2003	65+2	65+2	0	63	62	62	0
1939	2004	65+4	65+4	0	62	62	62	0
1940	2005	65+6	65+6	0	61	62	62	0
1941	2006	65+8	65+8	0	60	62	62	0
1942	2007	65+10	65+10	0	59	62	62	0
1943	2008	66	66	0	58	62	62	0
1944	2009	66	66+2	2mos	57	62	62	0
1945	2010	66	66+4	4mos	56	62	62	0
1946	2011	66	66+6	6mos	55	62	62	0
1947	2012	66	66+8	8mos	54	62	62	0
1948	2013	66	66+10	10mos	53	62	62	0
1949	2014	66	67	1yr	52	62	62	0
1950	2015	66	67+2	1+2	51	62	62+2 mos	2 mos
1951	2016	66	67+4	1+4	50	62	62+4 mos	4 mos
1952	2017	66	67+6	1+6	49	62	62+6 mos	6 mos
1953	2018	66	67+8	1+8	48	62	62+8 mos	8 mos
1954	2019	66	67+10	1+10	47	62	62+10 mos	10 mos
1955	2020	66+2	68	1+10	46	62	63	1 year
1956	2021	66+4	68+2	1+10	45	62	63+2 mos	1+2
1957	2022	66+6	68+4	1+10	44	62	63+4 mos	1+4
1958	2023	66+8	68+6	1+10	43	62	63+6 mos	1+6
1959	2024	66+10	68+8	1+10	42	62	63+8 mos	1+8
1960	2025	67	68+10	1+10	41	62	63+10 mos	1+10
1961	2026	67	69	2 yrs	40	62	64	2 yrs
1962	2027	67	69+2	2+2	39	62	64+2 mos	2+2
1963	2028	67	69+4	2+4	38	62	64+4 mos	2+4
1964	2029	67	69+6	2+6	37	62	64+6 mos	2+6
1965	2030	67	69+8	2+8	36	62	64+8 mos	2+8
1966	2031	67	69+10	2+10	35	62	64+10 mos	2+10
1967	2032	67	70	3 yrs	34	62	65	3 yrs

NRA= Normal Retirement Age

Then What Should We Do?

Or, as another example, if you are now 40, it won't be 27 years until you reach your present normal Social Security full benefits date. But under the proposed new plan, that would be 29 years, or 7% longer.

A second change that needs to be made in retirement dates is to increase the age at which a person can start taking *early* retirement. Right now that age is 62, as shown in column 7 of Table 14-1.

Column 8 of that same table shows one way in which the early retirement age could be raised. On this proposed schedule, the *early* retirement date would be raised in line with the *normal* retirement date, so that (starting with those born in 1949) "early" means *five* years less than normal retirement, instead of *three* years less (as it is now).

For example, someone born in 1951 (and therefore now 50 years old), would be able under the *present* plan to consider early retirement when reaching age 62, twelve years from now. Under the *proposed* new schedule, that person would need to wait 4 months more, until reaching 62 years and 4 months old.

A third change in when benefits start could then be to increase the penalty for early retirement by only *one-ninth of 1% per month or less.* This needs to be explained.

On the present plan, when someone retires earlier than their normal Social Security full benefits retirement date, the benefit is decreased 5/9 of 1% for each month for the first 3 years. If you retire 4 or 5 years ahead of the NRA, in those additional years the benefit is decreased by 5/12 of 1% a month (or 5% a year). Under the proposed plan, that 5/9 or 5/12 of 1% would become a standard 6/9, or 2/3 of 1%. That change would have this effect:

SAVING SOCIAL SECURITY (FROM CONGRESS)

You retire this many years ahead of when you would receive full normal benefits	Under the present plan, your benefits would be reduced by this much	Under the proposed plan, your benefits would be reduced by this much
One year	12 months x 5/9, or 6-2/3%	12 months x 2/3, or 8%
Two years	24 months x 5/9, or 13 1/3%	24 months x 2/3, or 16%
Three years	36 months x 5/9, or 20%	36 months x 2/3, or 24%
Four years	36 months X 5/9, plus 12 months x 5/12, or 25%	48 months x 2/3, or 32%
Five years	36 months x 5/9, plus 24 months x 5/12, or 30%	60 months x 2/3, or 40%

These are some of the justifications for changes such as the three just proposed:

In past years, a plan has been put in place that we now know is in serious financial trouble. We cannot ask just one generation, or just some of us, to pay to straighten this situation out. Right now, there are just 4 workers for every Social Security beneficiary, and in the next 25 years we expect that to change to be just over 2 workers, or maybe less than 2 workers for each beneficiary. Those who are now working but who are also planning on joining that group of beneficiaries can't walk away from their responsibility to contribute somehow to the solution of these problems.

The principal thing that these proposed changes would ask is not that people get less benefits, but that they simply wait a little longer for them. The changes in normal retirement dates wouldn't happen immediately, and as percentage changes (5% to 9%) they aren't large.

And, of course, the main reason that these changes make sense is that we are all living much longer. If we are, on average, living or going to be living 12 to 20 years longer than was the case when Social Security started, then we can certainly gradually raise the normal retirement age by 5 years (from 65 to 70) and the early retirement age by 3 years (from 62 to 65).

These 3 changes would clearly not solve the financial problems of Social Security, but they would be one sensible contribution toward a balanced solution.

One comment to those who would object to even these changes in retirement dates would be to remind them, "The alternative is that we probably won't be able to raise taxes enough to pay you what you expect anyway, unless you agree to be part of some changes."

Recommendation #5: For those who choose to remain with the Social Security retirement system, and who are working, their payroll taxes will increase immediately by 2.0% (from 5.3% to 7.3%), will go up an additional 0.7% (seven tenths of one percent) in the year 2005, and will continue to go up 0.7% every five years through the year 2025. (During this time, the 5.3% paid by the employer for Social Security retirement will remain the same).

In explaining this change, a member of the 40-and-younger workers might stand up and address older workers this way: "Almost all of us under 40 have looked over the facts and decided that, rather than pay for the retirement of others (including you), we are going to start saving for only our own retirements. We can do much better for ourselves that way. We have also gone over this with those who are already retired or ready to retire soon. We found out that they have also looked closely at the facts and have decided that they will be happy with any plan that simply makes sure that they get the benefits that they have been getting or expecting. So between our two groups, we know we have the votes to put through a change.

"Those of us under 40 are, however, willing to continue to have an amount equal to 5.3% of our pay come from our employers, to go to pay retirement benefits to those of you who stay in the plan, even though we would rather have had that become part of our paychecks.

"But we do need your cooperation on four points. First, we need you to agree with us that the Social Security trust fund money that has gotten into Congress's hands and been spent, is all to be paid back to the trust fund as soon as possible, along with the interest that Congress owes the Social Security fund on those loans.

"Secondly, we need you to agree with the rest of us that this is an exceptional window of opportunity, a time when there are still a lot of us working and building up a fund that can pay your benefits. But we need to act on this reform plan immediately, because the window of opportunity closes maybe as early as the year 2010, and every year between now and then counts.

"Thirdly, we need you to also agree with us that the money that should be building up in the trust fund in the coming years *also* needs to be kept out of Congress's hands and instead be saved for your retirement needs. The Social Security trustees will invest that money themselves, protecting it from Congress.

"Those are your three best guarantees that you will get your expected retirement benefits from Social Security.

"But the fourth need is that you will have to pay slightly higher payroll taxes. Those taxes will go up by 2.0% of your income immediately, and then keep increasing gradually over the next 25 years, so the maximum increase at the last is 5.5%. That is *your* additional price for getting the benefits that you had wanted *us* to pay for. You need to actually pay a little more for your own benefits. That's not asking much.

"If you don't want to do even that much, though, as your part in reaching a consensus on a new plan, then your alternatives are frankly to either opt out of the plan yourself or to face the prospect that the plan probably won't have enough money to pay you what you expect when you retire."

Then starting in the year 2027, the amount of payroll tax paid by *both* the employee and employer will decline every two years, on the schedule shown earlier in Table 11-1 on page 207, until the payroll tax for retirement is completely eliminated in the year 2047.

The point again is that, rather than having their youngsters pay for their retirement, these people who intend to receive the Social Security retirement income simply have to accept a greater responsibility to pay for their own benefits. That will probably not be a popular concept with those who have to pay for their own benefits, but the alternatives are that (a) their youngsters make the payments for them, or (b) there won't be enough money in the Social Security retirement fund to cover the benefits for these people when they retire.

Recommendation #6 is that the present laws about reduction of benefits for those who take *early* retirement and then work should *not* be changed. At present, those who take early retirement and then work have $1.00 in benefits deducted for each $2.00 in earnings above a certain limit. Offering benefits (even on a reduced schedule) years ahead of the Normal Retirement Age is of course an incentive to some people to begin drawing benefits before they normally would.

Leaving this reduction in benefits as it is, for those who want to start getting Social Security retirement benefits but still work, continues to tell them, "You can't have your cake and eat it too."

This penalty for both drawing Social Security and still working is meant specifically to discourage people from drawing Social Security benefits earlier than they normally would.

With the definite increases in life expectancy, and therefore the increased number of years during which retirees will receive benefits, Social Security simply cannot *afford* to offer increased incentives for early retirement.

The remaining recommendations then, of course, call for changes in the laws so as to give the appropriate tax advantages (similar to those now given to IRAs) to Personal Retirement Accounts, (or "Pension Retirement Accounts," or "Pension Savings Accounts," or whatever we choose to call them):

Recommendation #7: First, establish that for workers 20 or younger, there is in fact no longer an option of being part of the Social Security retirement system. Workers 20 years old and younger are required to drop out of the present Social Security system, no longer have the 5.3% deducted from their wages or salaries, and instead must put 10.0% of their pay into Personal Retirement Accounts.

Recommendation #8: And for all workers 21 and older, there is the option to either (a) remain with the Social Security retirement system as it now stands, and have increased payroll taxes deducted as necessary to fund that system, or (b) drop out of the Social Security retirement system completely and take total responsibility for funding their own retirements through contributions of 10.0% of income into a Personal Retirement Account.

This recommendation, of course, requires the establishment of all of the legislative limitations and controls that will insure that PRAs are invested only with conservatism and diversification, presumably only in bonds or in diversified mutual funds. The purposes of PRAs will necessarily be more conservative and controlled than will the provisions of IRAs, quite probably leading some people to want to use the tax advantages of PRAs only up to a certain extent, above which they would rather be investing with greater risk through IRAs.

Among the privatization options, these would be the selections:

The percentage would be 10%. Plans built around 2% or 3% are necessarily going to be complicated hybrid plans that leave the basic responsibility and control with the government, not with the individual. The 2% or 3% plans would certainly not provide enough income to entice anyone to leave Social Security altogether. Ten percent should be both high enough to be an incentive for those up to age 40 to leave Social Security and to provide future entrants into the system with far, far more retirement income than could ever be provided by the Social Security plan, mainly because it is personal *investment*.

The 10% should be mandatory, but with the provision that participants could opt out of making further contributions after age 60 or 40 years of contributions, whichever is earlier. Anyone wanting out any earlier (such as someone who is already independently wealthy) might be allowed out, on the condition of signing a release that gives up any right to any retirement income from the government. Few people would take that gamble unless they were quite sure about their financial status.

No credit will be given for past payroll taxes paid. Survivors term insurance will be mandatory for those with spouses and children under 18, at amounts that would provide coverage similar to what Social Security now provides. Individuals themselves, not the government, would of course do the investing, through special personal retirement accounts, with their restrictions.

No shared accounts. No guarantees of minimum benefits. No withdrawal of the funds for buying homes, paying major medical bills or sending the kids to college.

Special provisions in the event of terminal illness. Retirement any time after age 60, at the individual's own choice. Lump sum payouts would be possible, but probably not chosen, because of tax implications. No requirements to buy annuities. No forced payouts. Rewards to those who die after having worked at saving, investing and taking personal responsibility, by not taking this money away from them, their spouses, survivors or beneficiaries through estate tax.

Recommendation #9: Act now, because every day that we wait makes solutions less possible. We have only a limited number of years until the number of retirees surges, by the millions. The Social Security trust fund is currently growing by $100 to $200 billion — and soon more — per year, and this money needs to earn a real return, with all of this accumulation then protected for its original purposes. If that is done, it is the major means of financing the needed transition. But we also need every possible year, between now and when all these people retire, to raise some additional revenue to cover the expected costs of this greatly-increased retiree group. There is a one-time window of opportunity right now, but it is closing daily. It is essentially "now or never."

Also, the longer into his term that President Bush goes without educating the nation about the truth about the federal budget and Social Security, the greater the danger that he may be considered as being a part of the continuation of all the lying that has gone on before.

Finally, everyone of course needs to recall that the original objective of Social Security was never to provide for *all* of a person's retirement income. The objective was only to provide minimum retirement income as a safety net of some sort. As always, each person still has the personal responsibility to provide for the later years through a combination of (a) either Social Security or a personal retirement account, (b) other retirement plans, and (c) other personal saving, such as through IRAs and 401(k) accounts.

Solutions *are* possible

The above recommendations are at least one set of answers to the question, "Then what should we do?" They are quite likely not the same recommendations that you might come up with. But they should at least demonstrate that solutions *are* possible.

It's up to you

Our responsibility, as citizens of a mature democracy, is to actively participate in a careful and step-by-step national decision-making process that takes us together down that road to whatever solutions *are* right for all of us. Let your voice be heard.

Spread the Word!

For more copies of "Saving Social Security (from Congress)" —

— for individual copies
— for gifts
— for teachers
— for discussion leaders
— for book clubs

- **Quickest, simplest, for greatest credit card security, and for quantity discounts:**
  Order by calling 1-800-213-4181
  - 7 a.m.-7 p.m., CST, Monday-Friday
    7 a.m.-noon, CST, Saturday
  - We accept MasterCard and Visa
  - Shipment usually within 24 hours

- **Or mail your order** (with $16.95 + $3.00 shipping and handling, or total $19.95) to:
  Leathers Publishing
  4500 College Boulevard
  Leawood, Kansas 66211

- **Or available at your local bookstore or on the web at Amazon.com**

* * * * *

Ordering information is also available on our website:
www.sssfc.com
(as in "**S**aving **S**ocial **S**ecurity (**f**rom **C**ongress)")

Spread the Word!

For more copies of "Saving Social Security (from Congress)" —

— for individual copies
— for gifts
— for teachers
— for discussion leaders
— for book clubs

- **Quickest, simplest, for greatest credit card security, and for quantity discounts:**
  Order by calling 1-800-213-4181
  - 7 a.m.-7 p.m., CST, Monday-Friday
    7 a.m.-noon, CST, Saturday
  - We accept MasterCard and Visa
  - Shipment usually within 24 hours

- **Or mail your order** (with $16.95 + $3.00 shipping and handling, or total $19.95) to:
  Leathers Publishing
  4500 College Boulevard
  Leawood, Kansas 66211

- **Or available at your local bookstore or on the web at Amazon.com**

* * * * *

Ordering information is also available on our website:
www.sssfc.com
(as in "Saving Social Security (from Congress)")

Spread the Word!

For more copies of "Saving Social Security (from Congress)" —

— for individual copies
— for gifts
— for teachers
— for discussion leaders
— for book clubs

- **Quickest, simplest, for greatest credit card security, and for quantity discounts: Order by calling 1-800-213-4181**
  - 7 a.m.-7 p.m., CST, Monday-Friday
    7 a.m.-noon, CST, Saturday
  - We accept MasterCard and Visa
  - Shipment usually within 24 hours

- **Or mail your order** (with $16.95 + $3.00 shipping and handling, or total $19.95) to:
  Leathers Publishing
  4500 College Boulevard
  Leawood, Kansas 66211

- **Or available at your local bookstore or on the web at Amazon.com**

* * * * *

Ordering information is also available on our website:
www.sssfc.com
(as in "Saving Social Security (from Congress)")

Spread the Word!

For more copies of "Saving Social Security (from Congress)" —

— for individual copies
— for gifts
— for teachers
— for discussion leaders
— for book clubs

- **Quickest, simplest, for greatest credit card security, and for quantity discounts: <u>Order by calling 1-800-213-4181</u>**
  - 7 a.m.-7 p.m., CST, Monday-Friday
    7 a.m.-noon, CST, Saturday
  - We accept MasterCard and Visa
  - Shipment usually within 24 hours

- **Or mail your order** (with $16.95 + $3.00 shipping and handling, or total $19.95) to:
  Leathers Publishing
  4500 College Boulevard
  Leawood, Kansas 66211

- **Or available at your local bookstore or on the web at Amazon.com**

* * * * *

Ordering information is also available on our website:
www.sssfc.com
(as in "<u>S</u>aving <u>S</u>ocial <u>S</u>ecurity (<u>f</u>rom <u>C</u>ongress)")

Spread the Word!

For more copies of "Saving Social Security (from Congress)" —

— for individual copies
— for gifts
— for teachers
— for discussion leaders
— for book clubs

- **Quickest, simplest, for greatest credit card security, and for quantity discounts: Order by calling 1-800-213-4181**
  - 7 a.m.-7 p.m., CST, Monday-Friday
    7 a.m.-noon, CST, Saturday
  - We accept MasterCard and Visa
  - Shipment usually within 24 hours

- **Or mail your order** (with $16.95 + $3.00 shipping and handling, or total $19.95) to:
  Leathers Publishing
  4500 College Boulevard
  Leawood, Kansas 66211

- **Or available at your local bookstore or on the web at Amazon.com**

* * * * *

Ordering information is also available on our website:
www.sssfc.com
(as in "<u>S</u>aving <u>S</u>ocial <u>S</u>ecurity (<u>f</u>rom <u>C</u>ongress)")

Spread the Word!

For more copies of "Saving Social Security (from Congress)" —

— for individual copies
— for gifts
— for teachers
— for discussion leaders
— for book clubs

- **Quickest, simplest, for greatest credit card security, and for quantity discounts:**
  <u>**Order by calling 1-800-213-4181**</u>
  - 7 a.m.-7 p.m., CST, Monday-Friday
    7 a.m.-noon, CST, Saturday
  - We accept MasterCard and Visa
  - Shipment usually within 24 hours

- **Or mail your order** (with $16.95 + $3.00 shipping and handling, or total $19.95) to:
  Leathers Publishing
  4500 College Boulevard
  Leawood, Kansas 66211

- **Or available at your local bookstore or on the web at Amazon.com**

* * * * *

Ordering information is also available on our website:
www.sssfc.com
(as in "<u>S</u>aving <u>S</u>ocial <u>S</u>ecurity (<u>f</u>rom <u>C</u>ongress)")